THE GREAT CENTURIES OF PAINTING

COLLECTION PLANNED AND DIRECTED BY

ALBERT SKIRA

THE GREAT CENTURIES OF PAINTING

THE NINETEENTH CENTURY

NEW SOURCES OF EMOTION FROM

GOYA TO GAUGUIN

TEXT BY MAURICE RAYNAL
Translated by James Emmons

SKIRA

The colorplate of the title page:
Woman with the Fan (Edouard Manet)

FRANCE · SPAIN · ENGLAND · HOLLAND
UNITED STATES · ITALY · GERMANY

DAVID · INGRES · FRIEDRICH · GOYA · CONSTABLE · TURNER · BONINGTON

GÉRICAULT · DELACROIX · DAUMIER · COURBET

COROT · MILLET · ROUSSEAU

MANET · DEGAS · WHISTLER · FATTORI · JONGKIND · BOUDIN

MONET · RENOIR · SISLEY · PISSARRO

CÉZANNE · SEURAT

VAN GOGH · GAUGUIN · RYDER

TOULOUSE-LAUTREC

ONE OF THE REASONS why it has not yet been generally recognized that the 19th century witnessed a Renaissance of painting quite as authentic as the Italian Renaissance is our habit of regarding the 16th-century Masters as nothing short of demi-gods—sacrosanct, incomparable, infallible—rather than as human beings, men of genius certainly, but capable, like even the greatest, of lapses from perfection.

Yet the part played by the last century in art's long history was one of crucial importance; it did not merely extend the scope of 16th-century humanism, but entirely reshaped it. True, many important discoveries in technique had been made in the interval between the Italian Renaissance and the 19th century; yet, so far as aesthetic values were concerned, there was no notable advance. It was only with the coming of Romanticism that painting underwent a transformation at once radical and rich in promise. Speaking of Voltaire and Jean-Jacques Rousseau, Goethe rightly pointed out that while the work of the former marked the close of an epoch, that of the latter ushered in the dawn of a new world. And it cannot be denied that after reading Rousseau men saw Nature from a quite different angle. To him was due a wholly new conception of man's relation to the 'objective' world, both in the field of psychology and in that of art; a conception at once richer and wider than that of humanism, involving as it did the liberation of the individual Ego and the growth of an aesthetic of untrammelled sensibility. And, while allotting freedom of expression to the individual, it encouraged man to identify himself with nature in a new, romantic pantheism.

Reinforcing the romantic movement, the French Revolution, too, encouraged the artist to set up the concept of the free individual against the static conventions of the past. We must not forget that under the *ancien régime* painting was treated as a means, not an end; a means, above all, of shoring up the social structure, religion, the prestige of the monarchy. Under such conditions the artist was hardly more than a craftsman, bent on keeping up a reputation of proved efficiency in the service of his patrons. Thus his chief aim was technical perfection, in conformity with well-established rules.

The last twenty-five years of the 18th century witnessed the first strivings towards a free expression of the individual sensibility; the artist began to feel an impulse to exteriorize his responses, to body forth his private world, and to make good a new concept of art, its methods and its functions. There was no longer any question of the Aristotelian 'imitation' of nature; far otherwise, painting was regarded as existing in its own right and called on to exploit to the full, and wholly with its own resources, the infinite possibilities of this new-found field of action. Needless to say, such views met with the most vigorous opposition—especially as regards the assumption that painting's function was not merely that of illustration. Indeed this opposition has not yet died out. Even today we find, to our amazement, so eminent a philosopher as Alain writing with undisguised resentment: "We have come across some very odd theories according to which painting has a special kind of 'truth' peculiar to itself!"

Nevertheless at the end of the 18th and the beginning of the 19th century we shall observe—in the light of Goya's art—a struggle already in progress between the champions of an over-rationalized art and those who were moved by a compelling urge to paint, an almost physical need to give expression to the promptings of their hearts. This was, in fact, the chief endeavor of the forward-looking artists of the time; to set up intuition against the intellect, sensibility against the cut-and-dried, the living against the artificial and theatrical, and, in short, the true against that famous ideal beauty— *le beau idéal*—cherished by the dilettanti of the 18th century. This change of outlook accompanied the weakening of religion and the decline of autocracy. And the true nature of the 19th-century Renaissance became apparent when egotism got the better of altruism and individualism replaced the artist's social sense. The prestige of art-as-decoration was tottering; for to speak, magnificently perhaps, but to no purpose—in the academic style—is a procedure that is bound to pall, in the long run. The artist was discovering that he had a soul. Painting was by way of becoming a language of its own, with a vocabulary of new signs expressive of the artist's reaction to the aspects of reality. But now 'reality' meant what the artist re-created, after passing the visible world, as it were, through the sieve of his sensibility. Corot's "What we *feel* is as 'real' as anything else" struck the keynote of modern painting. The new reality consisted in the artist's personal response, in terms of the process described by Novalis: "It is less the subject that perceives the object than the object that enters into, and perceives itself, in the subject." And once the concept of this new reality had gained the day, it led to amazing results; each artist gave free play to his temperament, and a vast diversity of works of art resulted—none the less sincere for their discrepancies. From now on painting was a favored field for the egocentric activities of this new creative impulse, prolific both of aesthetic discovery and technical inventions. Intuition replaced observation and did yeoman service to the artist, eager to maintain his independence, as a defence against external pressure; likewise it stimulated that spirit of contradiction which often makes the modern artist seem so headstrong, not to say 'mulish,' imbued as he is with the fond but comforting illusion that he alone knows the truth, the only truth that matters, and has but to give free course to his magnificent, self-centered imaginings.

No doubt, as we shall see, false paths were followed, especially as regards the new 'reality' defined by Corot. Moreover now that the laws of perspective were being over-hauled, there was some uncertainty in handling them. In a general way it may be said that the artist, obsessed as ever with that eternal problem of rendering depth, applied himself to working out his own perspective, that is to say, ascertaining the best angle from which to observe that 'private universe' which now meant everything to him. Also, this quest of a new perspective entailed new technical procedures, and many such were tried out during the century. And thus each painter created his personal vocabulary, an idiom of his own, in keeping with his way of seeing the world and with his aspirations.

NOW *that we have seen the broad lines along which painting evolved in the 19th century, a further step seems called for: that of briefly sorting out the contribution of each artist to the new world of forms. And we shall attempt to show that, however intimately a particular mode of expression is related to the artist who created it, no work of art may be evaluated separately, for each, however isolated it may seem, is linked up with the great cycle of change which has marked the course of modern art. It seemed advisable to set out a brief summary of the 19th century, painter by painter, not by way of classification, always of doubtful value, but rather to bring out the positive character and the inevitable sequence of the forward steps made. We have sought to link up the artists and to throw light on the background and inspirations of the period, its impact on our own time and, above all, the destiny of its most important discoveries. We have made no attempt to sidestep such terms as classicism, romanticism and realism, but have tried to go beyond convenient and often arbitrary definitions in an effort to elicit that purer sense which colored signs take on under the great painters' hands.*

DAVID
1748-1825

*The End of
the 18th Century*

In his analyses of character, which heralded the realism of Géricault and Courbet, David belongs to the 19th century. In his neo-classicism, his respect for academic rules, and his rhetoric he belongs to the period of instability, currents and cross-currents, that set in after Lebrun. His attempt to stem the decadence of painting which took place in the last half of the 18th century marks the end of a well-defined period, which had begun with Louis XIV and is that of a state-controlled classicism. The operative factor in each case was far less of an artistic order than a rivalry between dictators of the arts. One of the two men flattered a powerful king, the other glorified the revolutionary leaders and then the Emperor.

Between the *History of the King* and *Le Sacre* there were great artists in France, but they had no connection with this Lebrun-David 'axis.' Though the terminal point for which David stands has historical importance, it had no bearing on the future course of painting. Nevertheless Lebrun made a sketch of the Marquise de Brinvilliers on the tumbrel, and David a 'snapshot' of Marie-Antoinette on her way to the scaffold; thus in each case a poignant glimpse of reality forced the artist to override his dogmatic notions of high art. At cross purposes between the theories to which he still adhered and a compelling urge towards freedom, David is justly given a place in the forefront of this volume; for he too shared in the aspirations and endeavors which were to be those of both the Realists and the Romanticists.

INGRES
1780-1867

Neo-Classicism

Such is the sensibility and freedom of his line that we are similarly justified in regarding Ingres as a harbinger of Romanticism; while his intellectual outlook and his quest of 'pure, unsullied beauty' place him in the long lineage of Raphael. Yet we cannot look at the *Odalisque* he painted in 1842 without being reminded of Seurat's *Circus*. In the former the sinuous line of the woman's body plays exactly the same part as the contours of Seurat's circus-ring, the horse, the woman rider and the clown, as regards the verticals and horizontals which in each case constitute the structure of the picture. In both *Odalisque* and *Circus* we find a harmony created by the 'analogy of contraries' which Seurat spoke of. It was a happy combination of these 'contraries' that gave rise to modern two-dimensional painting. Thus, while the work of Ingres had no place in the main stream of art from Goya to the Impressionists, it pointed towards the architecturally ordered composition of the opening of the 20th century. Indeed it might equally well be 'placed' immediately after David or following Impressionism. However it seemed to us more logical to insert it between Neo-Classicism and Romanticism.

The liberation of painting synchronized with the French Revolution; yet it owed much to foreign influences, those of Goya and Constable; it was Delacroix who set the seal on it.

GOYA
1746-1828

*The Birth of
Modern Painting*

With Goya we hail the coming of man set free from all restraints— social, religious and political alike. And now new sources of emotion were to change the whole function of painting; not representation but expression was to be the artist's aim. Goya did not deal in such obvious emotions or sensations as sorrow, fear or pain in their specific, definable state: that state which men had already come to terms with once and for all. What, greatly daring, he depicted was that which men feared to own even to themselves.

Intuitively he perceived that behind the conventional interpretations and classifications of the psyche, there is a human reality for which the sole justification of life consists in destruction. Man can but look on, aghast, at the follies and antics of a world in which joy and sorrow have no place, fear is not sublimated into heroism and suffering evokes no pity. It is this aspect of human reality that Goya expresses in his painting. Pascal said: "By space, the universe comprehends and engulfs me like an atom ; by the intellect, I comprehend it." And Goya might have said: "By its multitude humanity comprehends me and engulfs me, but I comprehend it because its reality is within myself." For it is himself he paints in his monsters, his sorceresses and his victims. Goya subordinated the subject to what he had to say. He took up expression at the point where Rembrandt had left it. He indicated essentials by rapid brushstrokes, played havoc with the rules of composition and lay-out and, as Malraux says, "invented dissonance." By setting painting free from all conventions, he opened the door to Romanticism, Realism, Expressionism. Many painters were to draw inspiration from the works of this visionary genius who in utter solitude explored uncharted worlds. In Delacroix' *Paganini*, in Daumier's *Drama*, in Manet's *Woman with the Fan*, we will see how much the 19th century owed to Goya.

CONSTABLE
1776-1837

*Open Air and Light
Toward Impressionism*

In Constable's landscapes we seem worlds away from Goya's tragic art, yet to the conjoint influence of these two men was due that new conception of the real which completely changed all painting from 1824 onwards.

When Goya's intuition revealed to him the analogy between the cosmic unity and the unity within himself, he had a vision of human nature stripped of all those conceptions which foster the illusions inherent in man's normal attitude to life. Cutting adrift from the particular, he identified himself with universal truth. For it is by intuition that the artist gets down to the real, and though the subject represented may seem to interpret an obviously subjective emotion, this is because the real has transcended Realism and assumed the function of a creative force. Constable's works express the sensations aroused by natural light breaking through clouds, mirrored on water, glancing over leafage. He paints a moment of light, a fugitive sensation that aspires to body forth the immaterial, the inapprehensible—to such a point that at first sight it seems to have no relation to reality. Yet what Constable expresses is very real; it is the sky. The moment captured is a particular truth, but the sky is the general truth. Constable painted the atmosphere, the vibration of the air, and when the English landscapists exhibited at the Paris Salon in 1824, it was a *liberation*—from David's hegemony. Thus while in Goya's art primacy is given to the reality of human nature and the subject represented is subordinated to it, in Constable's the sensation stems from a new reality, the source of light. Both the seeming objectivity of Goya's art and Constable's sensuous responses to the fleeting moment delighted the Romanticists, for these suggested liberties of execution matching their poetic flights of fancy. The Realists developed further Constable's keensighted observation of nature, the Expressionists found a congenial medium in the new subjects open to them, while Manet took from Goya the makings of that revolution in art with which we associate his name.

TURNER
1775-1851

A New Vision in Art

At last, with Constable, Turner and Bonington, Impressionism came into being. While no less sensitive to transient effects of light and to its disintegration, prism-wise, by the mists upon the Thames, Turner added a dramatic element, introducing into painting that stuff of dreams always implicit in reality. And in his last works he kept exclusively to themes that Monet was to favor: water, air and smoke.

BONINGTON
1801-1828

Painting in Bright Tones

Though Bonington spent so much of his life in France he was not influenced in any way by Gros or by the school of David. He had a keen eye for essentials and recorded them with easy mastery. The freshness of his colors and his boldness in handling them had much to teach contemporaries, especially Delacroix and Corot. In his landscapes we see a foretaste of the skies of Jongkind and Boudin.

GÉRICAULT
1791-1824

*Romanticism
and Realism*

At the dawn of Romanticism Géricault's art proves that this movement could not be dissociated from Realism or, more precisely, that they were simply two aspects of the same tendency in art. True, Géricault gave meticulous attention to the tortured bodies he portrayed, to decomposing flesh and contorted faces, for he wished to get down to the raw material of objects and human bodies; but he also aimed at giving a symbolic image of man's fate, and of the mysteries of life and death. Were it not for this poetic transfiguration, the realism and crudity of his depictions would be almost unbearable.

DELACROIX
1798-1863

Expression by Color

In the same way when, in his endeavor to express the heroic side of modern life, Delacroix applies the decorative and narrative procedures of such great masters of the past as Tintoretto and Rubens to dramatic events of the most 'topical' order, he also tends to sublimate his subjects on to a philosophical, historical or religious plane. Though his powers of observation were preternaturally keen (this is proved by the thousands of drawings and sketches by him that have survived), he always vivified them with his visionary imagination. Like Goya it was in solitude, when his creative impulse impinged directly on the outside world, that Delacroix did his best work. "It is almost always when one is alone," he wrote, "that one can get the best out of oneself; that is to say, feel the immediate impact of external objects, in terms of the relations between them and our own nature."

While Goya's subjects are bound up with humanity, those of Delacroix express a whole world by the interplay of colors only. "It is noteworthy," Baudelaire says, "and indeed of much importance, that when one looks at a picture by Delacroix from so great a distance that one cannot make out the details or even understand the subject, it inspires none the less feelings of sumptuousness, of joy or melancholy. It is almost as if, like hypnotists or magicians, his painting can make its thought felt at a distance. This strange phenomenon is due to the artist's marvelous coloristic gift, the perfect harmony of tones, and the affinity (predetermined in the painter's brain) between the colors and the subject. It almost seems—if this be not straining language unduly in an attempt to convey an idea of a somewhat subtle order—as if the color *thinks for itself*, independently of the objects it envelops. Those wonderful color-harmonies of his often make one think of chords of music, sometimes in a minor key; indeed the impression one gets from his pictures is often of a musical nature."

Thus Delacroix stands for the creation of form and the expression of movement by means of color and the division of tones—methods which the Impressionists and *Pointillistes* were to turn to good account.

DAUMIER
1808-1879

Humanity and Truth

In Daumier, too, Romanticism and Realism are closely allied; but a Romanticism and a Realism tapped at their source—that is to say, nearer to Goya than to Géricault or Delacroix. Daumier does not portray realistic scenes for their own sake, and the same is true of his literary and historical subjects. He painted the streets, the working class, the bourgeois with their foibles and ignobilities, the pettifogging lawyers and other queer characters haunting the Paris Law Courts. Before Manet and Degas he turned to scenes of contemporary life and in his economical drawing anticipated that of Toulouse-Lautrec. Daumier carried black-and-white to such a point that color became needless. Like Goya he might have said, "Give me a bit of charcoal and I'll make you the finest of pictures." In his lighting, his drawing with its shrewd analysis of expression, and his discreet use of color, Daumier belongs to the lineage which runs from Rembrandt to Van Gogh's art in his 'Dutch period.'

MILLET
1815-1875

The Song of the Earth

Millet, who of recent years has been unjustly thrust into the background, also possessed a keen sense for the analysis of forms and was thus able to build with volumes of the simplest kind. If we place his *Woman Sewing* or *The Knitting Lesson* between Georges de La Tour's *Magdalen* and Cézanne's *Old Woman with the Chaplet*, we see that the figures in each of these pictures are made up of the same simple volumes. Millet realized how effectively the rough cloth of peasant dress could eliminate the accidental and bring out the value of essential masses. Under the 'roundness' of the forms, we feel a solid frame and an incisive design which, by stressing angularity, does away with secondary planes. Pissarro and Van Gogh were, we may be sure, struck far more by Millet's constructive form than by his choice of subjects. Millet disliked being compared to Courbet and the latter seems to have paid little attention to him; yet, oddly enough, the youth with the basket in Courbet's *Stonebreakers* links up with Millet's *Winnower*. The two pictures were painted in the same year; Courbet's is one of the first of his works in which no trace of Romanticism is to be discerned and in which we find a real concern for the division of planes and volumes. From this time on, Courbet's work shows us everything Millet had been unable to express fully, hindered as he was by his desire to paint in terms of ideas and to make a symbol out of man. But the important thing for 19th-century painting is that Millet resuscitated and expressed basic forms.

COURBET
1819-1877

Expression by Volumes

Courbet analyses character and men's physical appearance without idealizing them; in his art romantic exuberance and the imagination have no place. After the great wave of freedom that swept the beginning of the century, and the emergence of Spanish, English, Italian and Flemish painters, Courbet linked up with a particular and permanent tendency which runs through French painting, from the Avignon Pietà, through Le Nain ('discovered' in 1862), and Chardin, and found a brilliant culmination in Cézanne. Though we are tempted to apply that somewhat ambiguous epithet 'realist' to this 'constant' of French art, it obviously does not fit the art of Chardin or Cézanne. As was the case with Romanticism and the realist reaction to it, the real plays a part in both tendencies; this indeed is a distinctive feature of the 19th century. This 'constant' manifests itself in the simplicity of the subject, which is usually taken from peasant life, does not range beyond the middle class, and has close contacts with the soil. The artist shares the emotions of his characters, he comes of the same stock and has the same respect for an orderly, thrifty, industrious life. He, too, owes his well-being and security to the earth, and he treats the family as a closed circle, a world in itself. Thus in a mood of intimacy, sparing of his gestures, the artist makes his pictures. The real is in the subject, but consists chiefly in the expression volume, that fully modeled volume which meant so much to Courbet, and [a] rendering which he applied himself so fervently that he foreshadowed [Céza]nne's 'distortions.' Both artists expressed density and weight, but by different [mean]s. Courbet's characters still wear the flowing garments of Chardin's ['hou]sekeepers.' In Cézanne's art, weight has disappeared, only volume remains, [and] his volume becomes two-dimensional form. Despite his reputation, Courbet [was f]ar from being a stupid man and he anticipated Cézanne's use of cylinders, [cones] and spheres as constructive elements, and already in mid-19th century [impar]ted to his work that 'solid and abiding' quality which was Cézanne's aim.

COROT
1796-1875

*A Balance
of Light and Form*

W[hile] the painters of light and those of form were following their respective pa[ths] another artist was advancing on parallel lines, but by himself and inde-pe[nden]tly; this was Corot. As early as 1824 we see him striking a happy balance bet[ween] form and light—which explains why, in this volume, we place him after Co[nstab]le and Courbet. For in fact his place is on the threshold of the period whe[re th]e problems of complete expression of form and light—and color regarded as a [qual]ity existing in its own right—were tackled by the painters of the second half [of] the century, the Impressionists-to-be.
"In [...]," as Venturi pertinently observes, "unaided, without a fixed program, and [in a] quite spontaneous way, Corot bridged fifty years of painting and moved from [Neo]-Classicism to Impressionism."
For [Coro]t is neither romantic, nor realist, nor neo-classical; he inaugurated what [has] been called "the landscape as a state-of-mind." So passionate was his love [of na]ture that all his work is composed of the impressions nature suggested to hir[m and] which he set down in all their purity and immediacy. Indeed he was the fir[st to] use the word "impression."
Wheth[er di]rectly or indirectly, Corot strongly influenced the future painters of the 'Arge[nteuil]' group, who came often to attach more importance to light than to for[m. B]ut there was one of them who never sacrificed the latter; this was Pissarr[o. A]nd while Cézanne realized the importance of Courbet's treatment of volume [he] was equally alive to the value of the balance between form and light ac[hieve]d by Corot.

THE SCHOOL OF
BARBIZON

The pai[nters] of the Barbizon School, amongst whom were Rousseau, Millet and (tho[ugh] very different from them) Courbet, saw in nature scenes more of a plastic a[nd a]rchitectural than of a sensorial order, and aimed at sumptuous and gran[dios]e effects. But they helped to bring into vogue the habit of painting in the op[en a]ir. Manet's *Déjeuner sur l'herbe*, which caused such a sensation in 1863, illu[strat]es this period of uneasy transition from studio work to open-air painting.

MANET
1832-1883

*Toward the Autonomy
of the Picture*

Between 1[860] and 1865 Monet, Renoir and Sisley contented themselves with seeking to [ach]ieve an equilibrium between light and form, volume and space. Courbet, [Rous]seau and Daubigny, while giving light a prominent role, put it to the serv[ice o]f form, while Pissarro, as we have pointed out, kept nearer to Corot's me[thod]s. He never wavered in his belief that light and form are not merely inse[para]ble but complementary, and that no solidly built composition can dispens[e wit]h either; there can be no light without form, nor form without light. For l[ight] does not merely serve to illuminate volumes; it *is* volume in itself. Never[thele]ss during the 'Barbizon period' color was not frankly, naturally rendered, it [rem]ained traditional; and while it limited the expression of form, it limited sti[ll mo]re that of light.

Corot was well aware of this, and it is why he used his silvery tones, thus approximating to what, apart from frankly stated color, can yield the maximum of light: black, white and various shades of grey. And so when Manet in his *Concert in the Tuileries Gardens* and *The Fifer* set out strongly affective flat planes upon grey backgrounds, the Impressionists-to-be were quick to see how much could be done by using colors without concern for visual truth. Soon they took to using these procedures for imparting more brightness to their canvases and, finally, for achieving the total conquest of light, making it shimmer on water and fall in broken gleams through leafage, clouds and smoke. It was Manet who set color free from representational service—and at the same time sacrificed the 'expressive subject.' Before the days of Manet, light, the human figure and the forms visualized in the artist's mind were expressed by him in the picture, whose object was to transmit the painter's 'message' to the spectator. The picture had its own reality in so far as it expressed a reality glimpsed by the artist, which enabled the spectator to perceive something his ordinary vision would not have shown him, yet which still retained some familiar landmarks to enable him to take his bearings. But in Manet's art the picture was no longer called on to transmit the real; *it was, itself, the real.* The evidence of the eye had lost its former infallibility. Thinking in terms of color became the painter's criterion of reality. By means of color the Impressionists created a new light, a light which dissolved all forms. Cézanne gave its maximum expression to the reality of forms and that of light, to the density of space and that of volumes, but without 'hollowing out' the canvas. In Manet's canvases the color is not called on to express light or form or emotion; the color *is* sensation, form and light. Nor does it aim at being expressionist. The *Execution of Maximilian* does not strike the tragic note of Goya's *Dos de Mayo. The Fifer* is not the portrait of a boy. In the *Concert in the Tuileries Gardens* patches of pink, blue and yellow dapple greys and blacks; the lay-out, borrowed from Courbet, registers the 'color sensation' produced by the crowd. Later on Renoir achieved the same effect, by means of color, in his *Moulin de la Galette.* Thus when Manet decided to follow Monet and Renoir to Argenteuil and to paint light, his pictures were colder than those of his friends—superb as was the color—and he was quick to realize that Impressionism was not for him. In any case, did not the inspired colorist that was Manet, who so boldly sacrificed the subject on the altar of color, create the most effective colors by means of black and greys—as Goya and Velazquez had already done? He is of the lineage of artists who did most to confer on painting its independence.

The new independence of painting was also due to the closer contact established between writers, poets and painters round about 1850. Under the auspices of Baudelaire, painting began to draw its subjects from contemporary life, that 'modern world' which Courbet, in his article in the *Courrier du dimanche* (1861), defined in this way: "Only its own artists, those who actually experience it, can depict the life of a period. I hold the artists of one century utterly incompetent to depict the life of a preceding or a coming century ... historical art is by its very nature contemporary." Thus we have the 'café-concerts,' the boulevards and the horse-races of Degas and Manet, those vivid scenes of contemporary life which were soon to become a favorite subject of the Impressionist painters.

DEGAS
1834-1917

Realism, New Composition

Although he took little part in the lively exchange of ideas between the different groups of painters, Degas, by his bold compositions and realistic drawing, revealed the extent to which the idea of investing the picture with complete autonomy had become the directive force in the art of the period.

IMPRESSIONISM

*Climax of the
19th Century*

It was on the Channel coast that Impressionism took definitive form; confronted by the sea and the immensity of sky above a low horizon, the painters came up against the problem of light under its most demanding aspect. And now the observations of Chateaubriand and Constable regarding the changes made on the face of nature by the passing hours, and the experiments that had been made by Jongkind and Boudin were implemented and verified by analytical methods of almost scientific precision.

MONET
1840-1926

*The Dissolving
of Form by Light*

Of the Impressionists-to-be, Monet was the one most attracted to the problems of light; and although in his beach-pictures of 1867 the luminosity is that of Corot, he had not forgotten the pointers Courbet gave him at this time and these we find embodied in *Camille*, one of Monet's finest works. While there the realistic treatment of the subject was concerned with the expression of volume, Monet was not long in developing a 'realism of light,' as we see in his *Women in the Garden*. If in this work the background speaks for Courbet's influence, the light is Monet's own, a light which, imparting a fine lifelikeness to the figures, at the same time attenuates their density.

RENOIR
1841-1926

*Color giving
Birth to Form*

Renoir, for his part—though he, like Monet, was fascinated by the broken gleams of light on the Seine—remained faithful to Delacroix and Courbet and was not long in reacting against a technique which at bottom rankled him, limiting as it did the possibilities of expressing form by color. Renoir became a kind of color-smitten Courbet, a lover of sheen and texture, not an innovator in the sense that Monet was, who with unflagging courage pushed the Impressionist experiment to its extreme conclusion—an experiment which brought to a dazzling close a century whose artistic personality was expressed in observation, analysis and an ardent love of nature. It was left to Cézanne and Seurat to effect their syntheses of form and color and to order them in terms of their relation to the overall pattern of the composition; to Gauguin to restore to color its constructive value; to Van Gogh to make of the picture a self-sufficient, expressive medium; to Lautrec to reinvigorate the power of linework. Modern painting—that of the 20th century—began with Cézanne, Seurat, Gauguin and Van Gogh: they were the harbingers of Fauvism, Expressionism and Cubism.

THE DAWN OF THE
20th CENTURY

*Construction and Color
Cézanne - Seurat
Van Gogh - Gauguin*

PAINTING IN THE NINETEENTH CENTURY

1
FROM CLASSICAL ORDER
TO CONSTRUCTIVE SENSIBILITY

DAVID · INGRES

BECAUSE of his respect for rules and orderly procedure, and the formal neo-classical style that he imposed even on the fashions of his day, David takes his place in that long line of artists which began with the century of Louis XIV and Lebrun, and whose aim was to ensure the worldwide triumph of an academic, immutable beau idéal *inspired by the Great Masters of the past. But, dogmatic as were his views, David was no mere pedant; his excitable temperament led him to involve himself deeply in the events of the day, and he recorded the characters and faces of the men who made them. In this part of his work, David showed his keen interest in the problems and anxieties of the new century and anticipated the realism of Géricault and Courbet. Ingres, however, tried—probably for the last time in history —to keep the classical school alive and to salvage that lofty notion of a pure and perfect beauty whose archetype he found in Raphael's art. In this we may say he succeeded only in so far as his art obeyed the directives of his instinct and the deeply sensual side of his nature. Indeed his passions always led him to overstep the limits he had set himself, and it was they that gave a ring of promise for the future to this last manifestation of the classical Reason.*

THE FRENCH REVOLUTION

A thorough-paced revolutionary of the 1830-1848 period and a recognized champion of the new art of his age, Thoré the art-critic summed up the influence of the events of 1789 on 19th-century art as follows: "Hitherto art was at the service of gods and princes; perhaps the time has come for art to serve mankind."

Obviously this precept had a twofold bearing, negative and positive. What was to be done away with was the art that had devoted itself to illustrating religious and mythological themes, to shedding its luster on kings and princes, or to shoring up established beliefs. The artist was now to 'serve' men in a very different way; by encouraging them, whatever their rank in life, to act as free, independent beings. Now that art was no longer called on to edify the soul, but to speak directly to the heart, its function was the free expression of life under all its aspects. Thus, for the aestheticians of the Revolution, it was not merely a question of inculcating ideas, sponsoring the new régime; they took a wider view and aimed far higher.

It is common knowledge that, unlike similar movements abroad (in England and America, for instance) which were chiefly of national interest, the French Revolution aspired to be worldwide and to free Man—and not the Frenchman only—from all the material, ethical and intellectual constraints imposed by the old world order. The principles enacted in the famous *Declaration of the Rights of Man and the Citizen*—those of liberty, equality and responsibility—made the artist likewise free to express his opinions and, what was more important, his personal sensibility, exactly as he chose. So now the artist was no longer to be a sort of flunkey in the service of the Ruler, but could follow the promptings of his inspiration on his own lines. He was invited to emancipate his individuality and to interpret his personal responses to life and nature; all the old academic rules were cast into the melting-pot. Thus David told his pupils, "Paint as you like, and not like me." What reality now meant to painters was not the servile representation of a theme usually foisted on them by others; they were called on to express emotions arising from personal experience of the life of nature and their own. "Men are born free and remain free." Thus the Declaration; and it applied particularly to the artist. Once, in the bad old days, La Bruyère had lamented: "All has been said; we have been born too late." But he had voiced merely the vain regret of a moribund social order. All had *not* been said—and anyhow were there not new ways of saying it? The art of the past had petered out in sterile repetitions drained of any vital significance, under the aegis of academic pedants who spent their time laboriously synthesizing the discoveries made by the Old Masters in flashes of high inspiration. The Revolution set out to promote new theories of art, ventures into uncharted fields of the creative activity—a thorough-going revision of aesthetic values.

But it was felt that limits must be set to this new-won liberty; and here the revolutionary aesthetic took what might seem in some ways a surprising turn. We must not, however, forget that a Latin race was aware—if only subconsciously—of the root

AND ITS INFLUENCE ON ART

meaning of the word 'revolution' (derived from the Latin *revolvere*); that it is applied, for instance in astronomy, to the *ordered* movements of celestial bodies. Thus, in France, the idea of revolution did not carry any suggestion of anarchy or 'eccentricity' (in the strict sense of the term), but on the contrary one of a just balance between authority and freedom. And, so as to justify their personal inspiration, artists of the period had recourse to orderly construction. It has been said of the political leaders of the Revolution that they had no clear idea of what they wanted, failed to exercise discipline and thus lost control of events. This certainly was not the case with the artists; they knew exactly what they wanted and built their works on firm tectonic lines. David and Goya, both fervent revolutionaries, never destroyed without a positive intention of rebuilding. Though circumstances led them to treat historical subjects sponsoring the cause of freedom (e.g. David's *Brutus*, Goya's *Riot of May 2*), they did not fail to go to Rome, to learn the basic rules of art from those Italian masters who set most store on order and due measure. Thus they were quick to realize that even freedom has its limits. Hence the fact that 19th-century art, erratic as was its course, never quite lost touch with tradition—if we use the word 'tradition' in its best, vitally human sense, and not as pedants use the term, meaning adherence to dry-as-dust techniques, the letter not the spirit of the past. Though the passing show of history is, as Renan said, nothing if not transitional, one thing is permanent: that immemorial tradition of the human spirit which respects and honors life under all its changing forms and endows great works of art with their immortality. And it matters little if the 'movements' that called them into being were short-lived, since these works renew their life in those that take their place.

Lastly, in this connection we do well to remember when the academic-minded (unjustly) attack Goya's and David's art—much as the French reactionaries, whether in exile or not, attacked the revolutionary administration—they are flying in the face of history. If the 19th century gave the world artists equal to the greatest of all time, it is because these artists followed instinctively that piece of essentially 'revolutionary' advice given by Goethe—a counsel whose application conditions both the historical significance and the permanence of all works of art: "Inhale but deeply the spirit of your age—and the work of art will come." In other words, the duty of the artist was to adjust the expression of his feelings and emotions to the events and trends of thought which shaped the world he lived in. He was to keep abreast of every new development, especially the vast changes that were coming over life, not only under the influence of the social and philosophical theories of the day, but as a result of the scientific discoveries of Chappe, Battencourt, Montgolfier, Galvani, Chaptal, Le Bon, and so many others. And to carry out this program, to make the most of the new era ushered in by the Revolution, the prime condition was that everyone, and not the artist only, should make good his new-won freedom.

DAVID AND THE LAWS OF ART

Artists who may justly claim to have given art a new direction come usually under one of two categories. There are some, gifted with a soaring imagination, who conjure up new visions of the world, discover sensations never yet experienced and devise original methods of expressing them. Others, less gifted, act the part of critics, they 'call to order'; that is to say, in times when art shows signs of lapsing into decadence or running wild, they sponsor order, measure and restraint. David belonged to this latter class; nothing of a poet, he was primarily a brilliant executant, a sort of spiritual adviser to the artists of his day, and he rarely departed from that schematization which was a second nature with him and on which he staked his claim to eminence.

This cult of a system ruled David's life no less than his art. We are told that he was a man who said little and thought

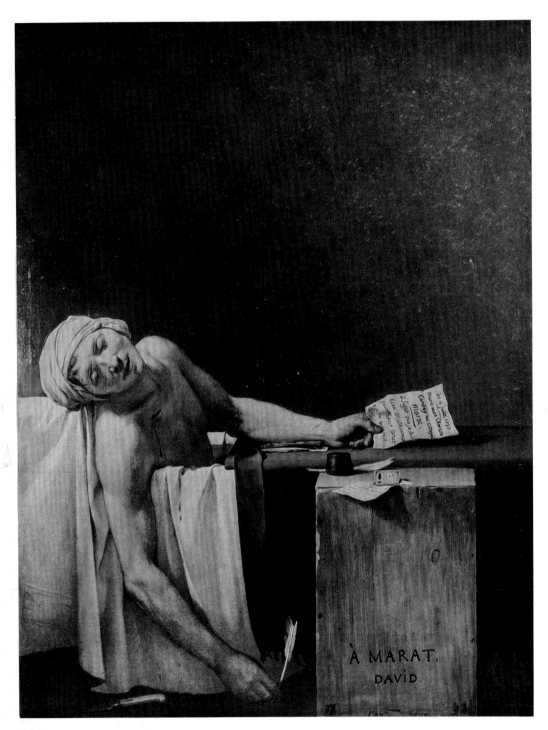

JACQUES-LOUIS DAVID
(1748-1825).
MARAT DEAD, 1793. (63 ½ × 49″)
MUSÉE DES BEAUX-ARTS,
BRUSSELS.

Whereas, in his historical works, David's chief aim is to link up with classical art, here we have a hard-hitting expression of his resentment at the murder of his friend. A critical eye may question the symmetry of the composition, so deliberately sliced into two parts. Yet, by this very means, a certain dramatic element is added to the work.

JACQUES-LOUIS DAVID (1748-1825). LICTORS BRINGING TO BRUTUS THE BODIES OF HIS SONS, 1789. DETAIL.
LOUVRE, PARIS.

As early as 1781, in his *Belisarius* (which bears the stamp of Poussin's influence), David showed a desire to break with academicism and move towards an art still more severe in style. Yet here, despite his active propaganda in favor of those republican virtues, good citizenship and stoicism, as exemplified in the story of Brutus, the artist has not entirely broken with the 18th-century desire to charm. We see this in the almost sentimental treatment of this detail, and we find it again in the group formed by Camilla and the other women in *The Oath of the Horatii*.

much. Even his friend David d'Angers, the sculptor, had to admit that he 'lacked charm, gaiety and wit.' The self-portraits (1790-1794) give us an impression of mingled shyness and enthusiasm, while the 1813 portrait shows a man handsome in a rather obvious way, with lackluster eyes and the look of a dogged, conscientious worker, but deficient in initiative. And, in fact, he seldom thought, or acted, for himself. He even was

JACQUES-LOUIS DAVID
(1748-1825).
PORTRAIT OF AN ELDERLY MAN.
(16½ × 14″) MUSÉE DES BEAUX-
ARTS, ANTWERP.

In his portraits David fell short of the expressive power of several other great 19th-century painters. Yet, despite his aversion for rendering 'expression,' he can, when he chooses, bring out the subtlest traits of his sitter's character.

1904

married by proxy—love of that sort hardly counted in his life. Still, after his fashion, he loved the working class, from which he came. The ruling ambition of his youth was to become a great artist, and he duly made his pilgrimage to Rome. Characteristically enough, he did not travel there alone, still less on foot (like Poussin), but was escorted by his teacher Vien. After his third failure to win a 'Prix de Rome' he was so disheartened that he tried to starve himself to death. He was always seeking guidance from such modish, if unreliable, aestheticians as Winckelmann, Emeric-David and Quatremère de Quincy. Later, his friends persuaded him to take a seat in Parliament, an honor that he did not greatly relish. He developed infatuations for the alarming personalities of Marat and Robespierre, and adored them as demigods—pending the rise of Napoleon. In fact, he had a congenital respect for the 'strong man,' whoever he might be; which is why the word 'imitation' came so often to his lips and figures so often in his writing. Thus we find him writing "Raphael and Poussin are sublime models to imitate," and, unlike Goya, he made hosts of copies, chiefly of the works of classical Antiquity. His political enthusiasms ranged from Robespierre to the Emperor Napoleon, and would no doubt have evolved still farther, had Louis XVIII thought fit to overlook his having voted for the death of Louis XVI and recalled him from exile. Nor should we forget that Tallien accused him of what today is called 'deviationism'; indeed he went to prison and narrowly escaped the scaffold.

In the last analysis David's limitations—his subservience to externals and unwillingness to risk looking beneath the surface—were probably due both to unsureness of himself and to the frigidity of his aesthetic responses. So total was his lack of interest in nature that he painted only one landscape, the view he saw perforce from the window of the place where, at one time, he was kept in custody. He made some pleasingly vivacious portraits; if they are no better than those by other 19th-century masters, the reason is that he usually left them in the condition of sketches. He would not have endorsed the saying of Ingres that when the painter has 'finished' his picture his work is not yet done; he has still to add the 'finishing touches.' Most of his figures look more like statues than like living people. "Giving expression to a face," he once said, "means having it make grimaces."

David's notion of the word 'freedom' had little bearing on his attitude to art; certainly he had not in mind the freedom of emotional expression we find in Goya's art. True, he told his pupils not to copy him, but to follow their own bent—but we should not attach undue importance to this seemingly liberal advice. Most art teachers say much the same thing; yet they do not hesitate to dismiss pupils who innocently take them at their word. Liberty, for David, was of a purely moral and social order, and the freedom he claimed was the right to express his opinions. Unfortunately this freedom served little purpose as his opinions were unoriginal, inspired oftener by others than thought out by himself. Always frigid in conception, his art progressed from youthful idealism to the lapidary realism of his *Marat Dead* and the *Death of Young Bara*. For a persistent refusal to come to grips with any deeply felt emotion is apt to lead to the style of coldly measured violence we find in David's art. Color never meant much to him; what most attracted him in Rome was the statuary, and especially the bas-reliefs, which he studied more from the angle of the archaeologist (he counted many archaeologists amongst his friends) than from the artist's. In marble he found a cold austerity that matched his temperament. At bottom he was an historian. "In painting the *Rape of the Sabine Women*," he said, "my aim was to illustrate an aspect of Antiquity."

For a painter this was certainly a singular aim, but we can understand its appeal for a man like David; especially when we remember how historical painters had the habit of dressing up the heroes of Antiquity in modern costumes. Making a point of choosing subjects that exemplified the revolutionary principles, he had no difficulty in applying to his art that neo-classical discipline which did so much to destroy the anecdotal frivolities of the previous age, whose disorder and laxity, not to say immorality, disgusted him.

More and more he played the part of a disciplinarian, until indeed his art became, as Stendhal put it, a branch of geometry. For geometry is an ideal stand-by for the artist who wishes to impose decorum on the scenes of life; and a stimulus for one who aspires to a formal, linear beauty. Even Goya admitted that something must be 'sacrificed.' In geometrizing his composition the great draftsman that was Goya found a perfect means of constructing form. And his essentially rational approach to art served him in good stead; his constructive methods sponsored a nobility, a formal elegance and a controlled dynamism which had salutary effects on the painting of his day, and which his followers turned to admirable account. We must not forget that Géricault never wavered in his allegiance to David, that Delacroix regarded him as "the initiator of modern art"; that Ingres always championed "the prestige of that great man David and his school," and that it was to Gros that he made over his studio when he went into exile. Yet the audacities of his pupils (all more daring than their master) greatly shocked David, who failed to see that they were merely carrying to their logical conclusion his 'geometrical' theories and in so doing giving them a broader application, breathing life into them.

We have suggested above the reasons why David's big works are apt to seem rhetorical, theatrical. In them movement is always attitude; he stylizes. His art reminds us of the pompous harangues of the orators of the Revolution. He is always striving after the grandiose and the sublime—but in cold blood. His composition is 'organized' like that of the great public festivals he stage-managed. As indeed might be expected of the man who bade Gros "Read and re-read your Plutarch." Still, though he made free use of gesture, miming, he never stooped to mere gesticulation; for there was nothing meretricious in his art and he was a draftsman born. Thus at times he attains dramatic intensity, but always kept in due control, thanks to skilled manipulations, a sleight of hand that rarely fails him. As might be foreseen, his palette is restricted—sometimes commonplace, not to say vulgar—and the tones (except in some sketches) are apt to look 'dead.' These limitations obviously derive from his cult of discipline. None the less he has a rare gift for the distribution of light, and with it he binds together the composition in a unity that forces our admiration. When he takes liberties with perspective this is to implement the 'effects' he wishes to make on the spectator, particularly so as to bring home to him that 'republican virtue' of austerity.

Thus David stands for all that in art combats the expression of purely personal emotion, allied with technical originality. We must not forget that he found Raphael too fantastic for his liking. Devoid of adventurousness and of any purely aesthetic impulses, he had no direct influence on any but mediocre and now forgotten painters. Paradoxically enough, David's art will always enjoy considerable popularity with that large section of the public whose approach to art is cautious, governed by the 'sound bourgeois commonsense' of which so much has been heard in France; those whose tastes are less concerned with real painterly qualities than with the pleasure they get from straightforward, easily understood scenes tricked out with rhetorical, would-be grandiose effects. Thus David has to be regarded as a pseudo-classic in the sense that Delaroche is a pseudo-romantic.

CLASSICISM AND ROMANTICISM

What exactly were these two outlooks, the classical and the romantic, that were now to confront one another?

Classicism stands for the pursuit of a perfection based on an ideal way of seeing things; its supreme aim is to embody the beautiful in its simplest, most abstract essence. It sponsors a purely spiritual, purely rational art in which form is represented, not merely as it appears around us in life, but after it has been passed through the control mechanism of the mind. Nature herself is no more than a starting-off point; she is idealized in terms of a set of principles whose control the artist accepts. Classicism is like a society regulated by settled rules of order and authority. It complies with a moral code which denies crude reality the right to permeate the thinking mind. We can understand why David was so fond of the term 'classical.' This supremacy of mind, which, to begin with, suited his

JEAN-DOMINIQUE INGRES (1780-1867). PORTRAIT OF GRANET THE PAINTER, 1807. (28 × 24″) MUSÉE GRANET, AIX-EN-PROVENCE.

Painted, like *Mme Rivière* (1805) and *Cordier* (1811), during the period when Ingres' genius was at the height of its power, this portrait is one of those in which he placed his model against a landscape background, drawn in with the precision of Van Eyck and a feeling for light as exquisite as Corot's. Studying the cravat, the folds of the coat, and the large flaps of the white collar, we see how Ingres, even when professing to do no more than copy nature, instinctively elicited a delicate linear rhythm from the reality before him.

temperament, had the additional merit of having been one of the progressive theories of the Revolution, that group of would-be philosophical principles which led up to the cult of the Goddess of Reason.

But all this theorizing ran counter to an art pre-eminently French in its devotion to immediate reality and the expression of life and the truth under all their aspects. We find many instances of this in art history throughout the ages, from the prehistoric *graffiti* of cavemen and the first illuminated manuscripts, by way of Fouquet, Clouet, Le Nain, Chardin and others—not to mention the Romanesque sculptors and the cathedral architects, up to the coming of Romanticism. And now, with the emergence of Ingres, began a kind of tug-of-war between the biddings of the intellect and the injunctions of the senses, with the fate of classicism hanging in the balance. Ingres, we may be sure, did not read Rousseau, whose reputation must have scared him. Yet even in the first works of this master the presence of a life-giving afflatus is evident. Breaths of tonic air flow round the figures; the artist has really looked at nature and his men and women have a sensual life of their own—possibilities which David never even dreamt of. With Ingres, classicism came to terms with life before passing away. The salutary notion of reconciling mind and matter now entered art and no more than a vigorous push was needed to send the old idealism into oblivion. Goya, then Géricault, then Constable, then Delacroix, launched that liberation of man which constitutes the Romantic movement properly so called.

Romanticism is always latent in men's hearts; we find traces of it in the customs, literature, sciences and arts of all ages. But now Romanticism came into the open. Its basic principle was the supremacy of the individual as a sentient being in his relations with himself and with the outside world. A deeper scrutiny of the 'self' brought to light feelings to which no one yet had dared give full expression. Certain sensations induced by natural phenomena gave rise to lyrical fantasies that sprang both from the imagination and from an increasingly acute observation of reality. Moreover, the problem of color set up the romantics against the classicists. For the latter held that the color should always be subservient to the design, whereas for romantics color was the life and soul of the picture and was in itself capable of building up form without recourse to contour-lines. Victories of the mind were vastly more fruitful when furthered by certain instinctual drives which the romantic refused to curb. This reliance on the faculty of intuition set in motion a creative activity by which man seemed to lift himself to poetic, superhuman heights, buoyed up by that comforting belief in his and nature's perfection which Rousseau was the first to promulgate. Classical idealism had been no more than an hypothesis, a sort of unilateral abstraction, powerless to implement the complex unity of human aspirations. And this was the noble ambition which Romanticism strove to realize in a mysticism, at once poetic and warmly human, that encouraged the new flowering of art.

Such was the change of outlook which led to the appearance of that galaxy of painters who gave the art of the 19th century both its diversity and its marvelous fecundity, pointing the way towards the new developments of the 20th century.

Towards the end of the 18th century English painting, too, was involved in the conflict between Classicism and Romanticism—that is to say, between respect of discipline and free expression of the imagination. William Blake (1757-1827) and Henry Fuseli (1748-1828), a Swiss who spent most of his life in England, chiefly asked of art that it should be a vehicle for the visions that came in dreams, nightmares and moods of feverish anguish, or for their conceptions of Utopias built on moral, metaphysical or purely imaginative lines. Men of letters rather than painters, they assigned to art the function of illustration. And though their works had some impact on the course of art history, we must frankly admit that neither of them was a painter of the first rank.

Henry Fuseli—whose name was really Füssli—is known as both writer and artist. He set up as a painter of nightmares, but his art is unconvincing and his visions seem not so much inspired as artfully contrived. He relied too heavily on system and never shook off the effects of an early academic training. Somehow his painting fails to arouse in us the sensations of horror he wished it to arouse, but remains rather childish; it 'tells stories,' effective in their way, but in a stiff and frigid style.

Blake was different. A profound and sincere mystic, with an uncanny sense of the supernatural, he claimed little interest in things seen, as he put it, by the "mortal eye" alone—a strange thing indeed for a painter to say. Some early critics thought to find a parallel between his art and the bogus classicism of Winckelmann and David, but this was certainly beside the mark. Blake's notions of drawing and color were of a rudimentary order, and, like all amateur painters, he was addicted to precision, high finish, rather finicking execution, and uniform tones—procedures tending to produce an illusion of classicism. Blake went ahead with little heed for any art but his own; he preferred drawing, engraving and watercolor to oils. On the whole his art is no more than the graphic handmaid, so to speak, of visions and fairy-tales whose suggestive power is never supplied by the drawing alone, and by the color even less. The creative element in his art is a mere by-product of literature; he interpreted not only poets such as Dante and verses from the Bible, but also, on occasion, apocalyptic myths already overladen with literary implications. He was always in two minds whether to express himself in poetry or in painting—sometimes, too, he included music; for he composed music for his *Songs of Innocence and Experience,* as well as illustrating them with engravings.

We find in Blake's art a simple faith, more of a Utopian than of a mystical order; it lacks unity and is always somewhat incoherent. His contemporaries thought him mad; but actually he was a genuine visionary, highly impressionable, and taking a childish delight in effects of fire and flame and contrasts of light and shadow, at their most extravagant. The deep sincerity of his inspiration, however, is beyond all question. Thoroughly romantic in character, Blake's approach to art calls for mention here. For, in the course of time, his work bore fruit; the Symbolists at the end of the 19th century and the Surrealists in the 20th drew inspiration from it.

No survey of Romanticism can possibly leave Germany out of account, even in painting. There can be no question, however, that German romantic painting never rose to the heights of power and originality that the same movement attained in literature. The great writers—Schelling, Brentano, von Arnim, Kleist, Novalis—have no counterpart in art and romantic painting remains a case apart in the expression of the German spirit. As a general rule, in the German romantic artist the German takes priority of the artist. Universality of mind is foreign to him. He does not aim at that total identification of man with nature whose starting point is a realist acceptance of sense-perceptions. The sensory element, with the German romantic, is kept in the background; it is to the cult of his soul that his inspiration gives the first response. His goal is rather an identification of the world-soul with the soul of man, a conception which prompts him to reject the interference of the senses. He seeks an anodyne for his romantic unrest, not in nature, but within himself. Thus, for him, painting is not an end, but a means of expressing his spiritual anguish, and satisfying his yearnings for an ideal reconstruction of the world. Nature he sees only with his mind's eye. Plastic considerations are irrelevant; when he is forced to give thought to them, he solves the problem by applying academic rules. And thus any notion of art for art's sake is ruled out; indeed, that notion was attacked with the utmost violence. Thus Kaulbach (1805-1874), a painter of allegories of a symbolical and didactic order, was inspired to make a famous picture in which we see a young woman shut up in an iron cage and guarded by a horde of monsters, while chivalrous knights engage in an attempt to liberate her. The young woman symbolized pure beauty; the monsters were the French romantics, while the bold knights were Kaulbach himself, his friends Overbeck, Cornelius and others, all given very realistic likenesses.

Some artists, however, like Ludwig Richter (1803-1884) and Moritz von Schwind (1804-1871), practiced a romanticism more sentimental in flavor, more idyllic, of 'the little blue flower' order. But in the main, their compositions stopped short with the anecdote.

Caspar David Friedrich (1774-1840), however, was a painter who did not entirely reject the data furnished by actual sight, though even he was imbued with the idea that the human should be submerged by the divine and that the eye need only serve the creations of the psyche. Poor all his life and dogged by misfortune, he took refuge in meditation and withdrawal into himself. And while the subjects of his pictures certainly reflect the turmoil within him, he does not let himself be bound by the academic technique of the age in his expression of them. There is real force and grandeur in his clashes of straight and broken lines, slashed through with slanting sunbeams. Other pictures by him, notably some of his landscapes, are bathed in a soft light which invests with a poetic glamor grandiloquently towering rocks and enormous trees. A painter of unquestionable talent, Friedrich united those two well-springs of romantic expression: imagination and the feelings.

INGRES AND SPACE

Jean-Dominique Ingres provided the link between Classicism and Romanticism. He was a would-be classicist, but the real turn of his mind was romantic. This he would have denied, but a look at the most sensitive, personal side of his output will convince us of it. And we shall see that, even while taking his stand for the disciplines of Classicism, he often gave way to those instinctual promptings that characterize the romantic artist.

In appearance Ingres was a portly little man of the South, with the "air of a notary about him," according to one of his contemporaries, or looking like a "Spanish padre in plain clothes," according to another. Rioux de Maillou talks of his skull shaped like a sugar-loaf, his flashing eyes, his nose disdainful even in his fits of anger, his dictatorial chin, his alleged resemblance to a balloon, and so forth. He lived simply and his married life was uneventful. Sensual by nature, he "frequently" remained faithful to his wife and was a good husband. His spouse was a fat, good-natured woman, with a talent for repartee. She was fond of chattering about "my Ingres" to whoever cared to listen, and hovered fussily about him like a widow gone idolatrous before her time. It was she who died first, well on in years, but the seventy-two-year-old painter soon filled her place by marrying Mademoiselle Ramel. Touchy to an extreme and arrogant into the bargain, he courted official recognition, and was well served in this respect. His pupils sometimes played practical jokes on him intended to gall his vanity, but he never got the point. A dutiful citizen, he treated the established order with punctilious respect. He had some setbacks at the start of his career, but his tenacity saw him through; for he was always ready for a fight, as harsh with his friends as with his enemies, who were numerous. His remarks were often biting, but at bottom he bore no grudge against those whom he attacked. He and his first wife made a comical pair indeed, but no one could deny the great little man's genius. He died at the age of eighty-seven, at the height of his fame.

One is tempted to parody the famous remark, referring to Lautrec's 'descent' from Degas, and say that Ingres was the best thing David ever made. And, indeed, Ingres was that master's greatest and most loyal pupil. There exists at the Louvre a sketch of the *Oath of the Horatii* signed by them both. Although at the start, owing doubtless to David's influence, Ingres' work had a touch of affectation reminiscent of the last years of the 18th century, it was never purely sentimental. On the contrary, his early pictures, the *Venus wounded by Diomedes*, for instance, show his preoccupation with purely graphic problems. Like his mentor, young Ingres was a great admirer of Antiquity, but not, like David, of its statuary alone. Any work which gratified his passion for line and contour fascinated him. Like Madame de Pompadour (who made copies of them) he loved cameos, and especially the figures on Greek vases, whose full, bold lines were his delight. Later on he discovered the Italian Primitives, painters either unknown or disdained at the time, an invaluable collection of whose works, now

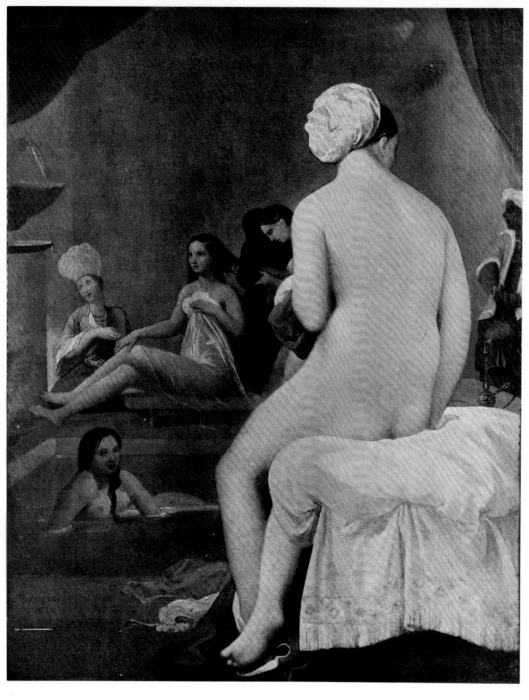

JEAN-DOMINIQUE INGRES (1780-1867). LA PETITE BAIGNEUSE, 1828. (14 × 10 ½″) LOUVRE, PARIS.

This picture is the link between the *Grande Baigneuse* (Valpinçon) (1808, Louvre) and *Le Bain turc* (1859, Louvre). The Ingres of the nudes, which he handles with such poetic feeling, is very different from the Ingres of the allegorical, mythological and religious subjects. Here the dike of his classicism has given way before the spontaneous flow of instinct. Whereas he plies his brush with sensual delight on the bare back of the woman, showering light upon it, the charming figures in the background are treated with a delicacy and reticence that charm and, in their context, come as a surprise.

at the Louvre, was bought almost for a song by Napoleon III. And it was these pictures that Ingres had in mind when he praised the "formless beginnings of certain arts," thinking back perhaps to David's advice: "Try to approach nature with the ignorance of a child." His life long Ingres was an *ingénu*, but, for all his ingenuousness, was strongly attracted by the elegance of the School of Fontainebleau and the drawings of Primaticcio; by François Clouet's *Bain de Diane* and *Femme à la Toilette*, as well as by that master's portraits, whose pure and lifelike style he himself was to equal. In all Ingres' works, we feel a partiality for refined and delicate contour-lines, verging on the precious; yet in his art they are not in any sense contrived, but the expression of a real sensibility.

Ingres disclaimed idealist and realist views alike, but was fond of using the word 'classical.' He professed that his aim was to paint "history on the grand scale," an odd remark to come from the painter of the *Odalisques*; yet this clearly states the goal he set himself but never quite reached. For it is always rash to feel too sure of the superiority of the intellect as against the emotions. His father was a painter and musician. That famous *violon d'Ingres* was not a mere ostentatious hobby as some have thought; actually in his youth he played in the theater orchestra at Toulouse. Thus there was nothing amateurish about him; and he learnt the rudiments of art at an early age, readily submitting to the discipline that this involved. All his life Ingres was a staunch believer in order, and accepted with a good grace the rigors of the

JEAN-DOMINIQUE INGRES (1780-1867). ODALISQUE WITH SLAVE, 1842. (28×39″) WALTERS ART GALLERY, BALTIMORE.

In 1840 Ingres completed a first version of this picture in which the foreground is identical with this, but the background is closed off by a wall instead of opening out on to a garden, as here. This is one of the compositions for which Ingres was most severely taken to task by his contemporaries. "The navel of the odalisque is a mere hole in her side; the thigh, leg and foot of the servant-girl playing an instrument are indescribable," was T. Silvestre's comment—rather an academic view for a champion of romanticism to take. Today we admire the bold handling of the lines of the woman's body, and its poetic overtones, surprisingly romantic for a professedly classical painter.

academic curriculum. He took his stand, however, against the *beau idéal* so dear to Quatremère de Quincy and asserted that "style is nature." A remark giving more than a hint as to the true bent of his mind. Yet where can we find a trace of "nature" in his mythological allegories or in the *Apotheosis of Homer*, in which he could hardly bring himself to include Shakespeare? This is, in fact, the weakest side of his work; but it is accounted for by his quest of an 'ideal' which he never reached. Doubtless he had some inkling of this, and the thought rankled. Of course—and this, too, should be noted —he claimed that art's salvation lay in respect for nature as she was seen through the eyes of Raphael and the Greeks. Ingres genuinely loved nature. Thus he always wavered between an acquired intellectual discipline, on the one hand, and an innate realistic bias, so typically French, on the other.

When we examine the nudes in the *Odalisques, La Source* and *Le Bain turc* (Plates) we seem to see a clash between instinct and reason, the outcome of that organic driving force which made him paint. Yet Ingres never squarely faced the existence of this instinct. He was for ever baffled by the hidden drives within him whose origin—at least as concerns art—he never clearly discerned. He was vexed by these 'interferences' and shocked at the uprush of instinctual forces in whose working any true romantic would have seen the hand of fate—or Providence. Although in his portraits—and no master has done better ones—he is lavish of details, contour-lines and linear patterns whose wealth borders on prodigality, none the less, true Frenchman that he is, he uses them only with an eye to producing a finished work, and this with an almost mechanical precision, verging on the miraculous. On the other hand, when he paints a nude woman he seems another man, a man entranced; the contour-lines envelop the body in voluptuous curves, and he does not attempt to check their soaring flight. Instinct has so thoroughly dethroned the rational that the plastic sense itself becomes instinctive. It is then that he conjures up a play of forms unknown to his religious and historical compositions.

Obviously a vision of nature on the lines of Courbet's or Corot's, a pantheism on the lines of Rousseau's, was not to be expected of Ingres who, in point of fact, did no landscape painting. It is rather in the handling of the contour-lines of the nudes that we find an indication of the unrest that always stirred within him. Although he was by no means fond of color for its own sake (he never gave a thought to 'complement-aries'), his wonderful tints develop at times a concentrated warmth and luminosity —though this, we must admit, is exceptional in his work. "Color—a trivial amenity," he is reputed to have said. His unworthy pupil, Amaury-Duval, put his finger on this when he spoke of Ingres' "insensitivity." We cannot but regard many of his portraits, whether in colors or in black-and-white, as unquestionable masterpieces, but we have to admit that this is all they are, that is to say works that have definitely 'come off,' but have nothing to give the future but object lessons. It is usually in the nudes that we see his genius at its best, that genius which always puzzled him, for it seemed to be leading him astray from what he deemed perfection. It is rightly said that great artists never really know what they are doing. So it was with Jean-Dominique Ingres.

2
TOWARD THE DISCOVERY
OF A NEW WORLD:
MAN AND LIGHT

GOYA - CONSTABLE
TURNER - BONINGTON

GOYA *emancipated painting from all moral obligations, from all political, religious or social disciplines. He was the first painter to go beyond the expression of sensations and emotions and try to get down to the underlying truth of human nature. So as to enter into immediate contact with the dark forces that possessed him, he invented new short-cuts, so to speak. Isolated by his infirmities from the world he had so ruthlessly unmasked, he developed as it were a multiple personality and identified himself with all living beings. This new, revolutionary awareness of man had its counterpart in the art of Constable in a new attitude to nature. Nature has as many modalities as the light that bathes her and seeps into her calls forth. This natural light is ever-changing, ethereal; and, for Turner, the stuff that dreams are made of. And these two great discoveries imparted to the world of visual experience new overtones and opened vistas on infinity. Man became the lord of creation, and nothing was forbidden him.*

SOLITUDE OF GOYA

For several reasons Francisco Goya may justly be said to have inaugurated, and indeed inspired, most of the great changes that came over painting in the 19th century. For one thing his work was the most forceful expression of the artist's personal freedom that art had ever known; then, again, it was a ruthless satire of the whole social order soon to be swept away by the French Revolution, as well as an indictment of those ancient, deeply rooted Spanish institutions which the great artist seemed to be making it his business to overthrow.

Yet we may question whether, however justifiable the cause served by his tirades, it was any, strictly speaking, political end he had in view; was it not, rather, a profound dissatisfaction with the world at large (that congenital Spanish *malaise*) that made him so eager to destroy all around him, even if he too were crushed under the ruins?

Indeed Goya's personality is something of an enigma and it is hard to unravel its true purport from the known facts of his strangely checkered life. Yet in his case it is particularly desirable to know something of the man himself before attempting to appraise the artist.

The self-portrait shows us a man with a strong face, a faintly disillusioned smile, a manner at once resolute and uneasy, a curious combination of robustness and ill health. Indeed in him we seem to see two personalities, a hopeless invalid's and a would-be fit man's, vying with each other, and this may explain that high nervous tension and morbid sensitivity which, fused with genius, characterize Goya's art. We know that in the course of his long life he had two serious illnesses, but of an unspecified nature; perhaps it was thought best to draw a veil over them. He was dogged by ill luck; his eyesight gave him trouble and, when he was forty-seven, he became deaf—which must have complicated his relations not only with his wife and family (he had some twenty children) but also with the Dulcineas of his many extra-conjugal 'affairs.' It may have been due to these handicaps that he became a soured, crochety man; but, also, there seems to have been an anarchic strain in his make-up which led him to question everything with an almost inquisitorial fervor, tinged sometimes with mysticism. His tormented spirit was always 'hot for certainties,' always seeking for some ultimate truth of whose existence he never doubted, but which always eluded him. Meanwhile of one thing he was certain: that he must do away with all aesthetic principles and technical procedures which would cramp the free expression of his emotions and imagination. This may explain the protean changes in the career of this remarkable man—now courtier, now fashionable artist working on tapestry cartoons or decorating the residence of the Duchess of Alba (who showed him special favor), now misanthropist, now revolutionary and violent denouncer of wars, massacres and the follies of the age, scarifying them with typically Spanish virulence. He came of humble extraction (his father was a gilder); it was all that he could do to win a second prize in an official competition. Many tales are extant of his scapegrace youth: how he got into trouble with the Inquisition (hardly surprising in a country where, little more than a hundred years before, an artist of Velazquez' stature had had to paint his only nude in secret, we are told, with the protective collusion of the king), how he was stabbed in brawls, narrowly escaped being sentenced to death for breaking

into a nunnery in Rome, and the like. Then, suddenly, when he was thirty-one, his luck turned. He was admitted to the Academy and later became King's Painter at the court of Charles IV. During the French occupation he had no compunction about 'collaborating' (as Joseph Bonaparte's official painter), but meanwhile carried about with him a knife bearing the inscription 'Death to the French!' Later, after the French defeat, he was Court Painter to King Ferdinand VII. Near the end of his career he decided he would be safer out of Spain (what exactly he feared has never been made clear) and obtained some weeks' leave

FRANCISCO DE GOYA Y LUCIENTES (1746-1828). MANOLA. DETAIL. PRADO, MADRID.

In 1819 Goya had bought a house near Madrid which his neighbors came to call the "Deaf Man's House." Inside, on the walls, he painted a picture sequence in somber, murky tones, whose subjects—the Fates, witches' sabbaths, peasants coming home from the fair, Saturn devouring his children—gave ample scope to his eerie imagination. This woman leaning against a rock is a far cry from the *beau idéal* dear to the artists of Goya's time. He does not flatter his model but, inspired by his intense love of life and his satiric instinct, he shows her as she really is.

FRANCISCO DE GOYA Y LUCIENTES (1746-1828). THE RIOT OF MAY 2 AT THE PUERTA DEL SOL. (105 × 136″)
PRADO, MADRID.

In April 1808 French troops occupied Madrid, while, at Bayonne, the old king, Charles IV, renounced his throne. On May 2 a riot broke out in the capital and was ruthlessly put down by Murat's troops. An ardent patriot, Goya set out to record for posterity one of the fierce street-fights during which the Spaniards mistook Napoleon's Mamelukes for Moors, their traditional foes. Critics and fellow-painters found fault with the picture at the time, complaining that the drawing was inaccurate and the color falsified. Be this as it may, the driving force of this work compels our admiration and is a prelude to the passing of the bogus classicism of the day.

of absence from the King. But he never returned to live in his country, and died in exile at the age of 82. If there is much to baffle us in Goya's career, with its spectacular ups-and-downs, this much is clear: that he was a very exceptional man and this singularity did much in the shaping of his genius.

FRANCISCO DE GOYA Y LUCIENTES (1746-1828). THE SHOOTINGS OF MAY 3, 1808. (105 × 136″) PRADO, MADRID.

This tragic scene recalls the invasion of Spain by the French armies under Napoleon. In the night of May 2-3, the French general Grouchy had some captured rioters taken out and shot. Particularly telling is the contrast between the dense mass of soldiers, the row of parallel rifles, and the group of terror-stricken prisoners. Instinctively we compare this picture with the celebrated canvas by Manet, painted in 1867, depicting the execution of the Emperor Maximilian in Mexico, and with Picasso's recent picture called forth by the fighting in Korea. Goya did not react to war with the coldness of the classicists, for whom it was but a pretext for skillful displays of virtuosity. His rebellious soul gave vent to all its pent-up hatred for ambition, tyranny, man's cruelty to man.

Perhaps we should do best to regard him less as a painter born than as a man who used painting as the language for expressing his views on a world that he had vague dreams of remolding to his heart's desire. There is a Spanish saying that "Spaniards never know what they want, but they know quite well what they *don't*

FRANCISCO DE GOYA Y LUCIENTES (1746-1828). THE PROCESSION OF THE FLAGELLANTS, C. 1794. (18 × 29″)
ACADEMY OF SAN FERNANDO, MADRID.

Although Goya treated this ceremony almost like a masquerade, he was not prompted by any anti-religious bias. The picture is divided into two scenes one of which, full of devout feeling, shows worshippers kneeling before the radiant figure of the Virgin, and has a deeply moving quality. The other depicts the flagellants and the flagellated in a manner verging on caricature—nevertheless, this scene, too, is moving, if in a different way; indeed we feel the artist has been carried away by the mystic fervor of the penitents. This work owes its intense lifelikeness to the fact it is a kind of 'snapshot.' And thereafter Manet was to learn something from these powerful contrasts of light and shade.

want." In this respect Goya was a true Spaniard. It also explains his desire for freedom, his abrupt changes of direction, his ambivalence in coping with the vicissitudes of a life which we can hardly be sure he would have wished less stormy. Thus one of his characteristics is spontaneity; he never pauses to reflect, but leaps before he looks. He never set down his ideas on paper; a few letters to friends are all we have. Some have said that Goya was ruled by his caprices, as a result of being so much wrapped up in himself. His attitude seems to have been that of a great hater rather than that of a revolutionary. What he resents, everything that makes him suffer, he regards as evil: crime, ugliness, stupidity. Because these ruffled the peace of mind for which this victim of his nerves was always craving in his heart of hearts. In that wonderful series of engravings in which he lays bare his deepest feelings we have not so much a political message as the expression of a temperament that can never find repose. For Goya was well aware that crimes, stupidity and vain pretences are common to all epochs, revolutionary included. Thus in his art propaganda (usually of small artistic value when intended to appeal to a large, undiscriminating public) counts for little. Always the artist took precedence of the partisan, as becomes clear when we examine his technique: that exquisite linework emphasizing the contours, stressing relief in exactly the right places, defining the modeling, fixing positions so strongly yet discreetly, with such luminosity and originality. No doubt Goya in his angry moods found all things more

or less odious—the view of the hypochondriac, but sometimes also of the genius. One feels he 'has it in for everything,' and on the occasions when he smiles, smiles sourly. Sometimes, too, sadly conscious of his powerlessness to change the world that is, and haunted by that Spanish sense of *nada* —the nothingness of all—he conjures up, like another Prospero, a world of which he is the absolute lord and master. A peculiar 'anxiety' (wellknown to modern psychology) led him often to depict flying men and animals —forms of an elementary surrealism— symbolizing, perhaps, his longing to escape from life's ugliness, no less than from the conventions foisted on him by the academicism of his age.

Though in Madrid and Rome he visited museums and studied the great masters, he never copied; and though he would sometimes spend a whole day gazing at a masterpiece, analysing and

FRANCISCO DE GOYA Y LUCIENTES (1746-1828). THE BEWITCHED, 1798. (16 × 11 ½″) REPRODUCED BY COURTESY OF THE TRUSTEES, THE NATIONAL GALLERY, LONDON.

Goya's anguished spirit was for ever probing into the mysteries of the universe. A true Spaniard, he was full of superstitions and took a special pleasure in diabolic evocations of this order. Have we here a priest trying to fight down the promptings of the devil? The theme is expressed in an original, highly imaginative composition, implemented by dramatic effects of lighting that simplify and bind the parts together. As Goya himself said: "It won't do for my brush to see with greater insight than I do."

appraising it, he refused to adopt the style or mannerisms of any other painter and asked all of his intuition. In Rome he met David, but the two men's friendship was short-lived; David's cult of classical Antiquity repelled him. For he was little drawn to historical or religious subjects; he preferred scenes taken from everyday life. And his highly personal technical procedures, too, were anticipations of the painting of the 19th century. "In nature," he wrote in a letter to a friend, "there are no lines; I see only advancing and receding planes, reliefs and recessions. Nor do colors exist in nature. Give me a piece of charcoal and I will make you a picture; all painting consists in *sacrifices*." Prophetic remarks, which were to make a deep impression on Delacroix, Courbet and Baudelaire.

The composition, too, in Goya's pictures took an extremely original form. Obviously it does not stem from any preconceived program; yet it is always perfectly balanced, and this balance owes nothing to any of the classical prescriptions for 'harmonious proportion.' True, in several of his works we find the famous golden section, traditional norm of absolutely satisfying formal relations, but he lit on it intuitively, much as a good cabinet-maker lights on the best proportions for a sideboard, or a papermaker for the format of his sheets. Composition, with Goya, has something of the photographic snapshot; he 'takes' the aspect of his subject seen with his mind's eye, in a flash of intuition. And since this sudden vision is usually inspired by some emotion of a dramatic nature, it has a dynamic quality which impels the artist to its immediate rendering. He has no time to 'arrange,' nor indeed has he the slightest wish to do so.

The truth is that Goya was convinced his instinct could never play him false, and rarely troubled his hand with problems of composition. Like the sculptor drawing forth directly from a block of marble the statue immanent within it—without pausing to make a model—Goya seems to draw forth from his imagination the picture ready-made. Thus he needed no preliminary sketches; even his drawings have nothing of the sketch about them; they are finished works.

During a period of revolt, a spiritual crisis that played havoc with his peace of mind, Goya felt an irresistible desire to escape from everything and everybody, though he knew that solitude well might mean an aggravation rather than an alleviation of his distress. He bought a house in the country, hidden amongst big trees—his neighbors called it *La Quinta del Sordo (The Deaf Man's House)* and there, upon the big bare walls of his studio and of the dining-room, he slashed, rather than painted, a series of extraordinary, intensely harrowing compositions, in black and white.

In these *picturas nigras* as they came to be called, which include *Saturn devouring his Children,* the *Fantastic Vision,* the *Old Man Drinking Soup,* it is a terrifying world that Goya shows us, teeming with witches, giants, men with skulls for heads, rendered in clashing volumes, splashes and smears of black. As regards the drawing, he casts all realistic accuracy to the wind.

As might be expected, academic-minded critics found fault with his draftsmanship, accused his colors of lacking veracity, and ridiculed his figures posed askew like Cézanne's bottles; his horses, too, were a standing joke amongst the dilettanti of the day. His figures and his portraits of kings and queens, so magically true to life, have been taxed with vulgarity and alleged to be badly constructed. The truth is that he painted in terms of masses laid out in a wholly new manner, often employing low-pitched tones with elaborate, strongly emotive contrasts, involving very subtle relations between the tones. It has been said that he excelled Velazquez in the handling of neutral tints and *grisaille*, which he preferred to brilliant color effects. His is an art of marvelous translucencies, broken gleams and glittering highlights, warm, vibrant colors, delicate silvery sheens. He laid on his paint sometimes with the palette-knife, sometimes with his painter's sponge, sometimes with his fingers—and always with a rare, deeply moving sobriety. True Goya, nature-lover as he was, sought to express reality, but he never lapsed into realism; for he refused to tie himself to any aesthetic theory and preferred to be a law unto himself.

Briefly, Goya's practice may be summed up as a reaction against the official painting of the 18th century—but not a classical reaction as was David's; total freedom accorded to the expression of his personality (already imbued with the Romanticism of the next generation); frank acceptance of the implications of 'pure' painting as against the pictorial conventions of the past; the creation of a new tectonic handling of forms (whose influence was destined to be far-reaching); outlines defined by masses; and, lastly, a novel, highly personal vision of reality.

To these new conceptions, aesthetic and technical, which he so eloquently put into practice in his art, Goya owes his undisputed eminence not only as one of the greatest painters of all time but as the harbinger of the 19th-century renaissance.

THE ENGLISH LANDSCAPE

Despite the persistent hostility shown by the Anglican clergy to painting (that 'instrument of popery'), England's contribution to 19th-century art was to be an important one, even providing the basis of a whole branch of modern painting. The love of the English for nature is proverbial, and this is the beginning of the romantic attitude. Indeed the word itself, 'romantic,' is a relatively old one in English, being in current use in England long before it was taken over by continental *littérateurs* and critics. English painters have always shown a sensitive appreciation of nature, even when treating landscape merely as a decoration. Once, by way of a joke, Hogarth engraved a landscape full of lively figures, but riddled with amusing violations of the laws of perspective. Here we surely have a slyly satirical attempt to restore to nature a life and interest lost when artists used it for merely decorative ends. This new turn of things, of which we find no counterpart in French painting, took place in the 18th century.

In his portraits Joshua Reynolds (1723-1792) was fond of placing his models before a landscape background in which sky, trees and foliage are almost as much alive as the figures. Gainsborough (1727-1788) did the same in his portraits, and in fact began his career by doing landscapes of the delightful Suffolk countryside. So that in England, even though he kept to the traditions of the Dutch landscapists, Gainsborough inaugurated a kind of painting never to be surpassed anywhere for the simplicity and truthfulness of its expression, drawn from the resources of a very subtle palette.

Another painter of the day, Richard Wilson (1713-1782), who spent much time in Italy, sought to combine Dutch realism with the monumental side of Italian landscape. His rural compositions are not unmoving; in them we feel the beginnings of a direct participation of the artist in the life of nature. From Wilson's time on, landscape assumed increasing importance in English painting. John Crome (1768-1821) devoted himself to landscape and founded the Norwich school of painters. With him landscape-painting began to break free from the conventional and academic. Obviously he drew his inspiration from the Dutch Masters, but he put much of himself into his work as well. Crome had been in Paris and painted there a *Boulevard des Italiens*. But though his feeling for nature was far from being as strong as Constable's, he did not merely use it as a decorative element. He liked big trees, vast skies, hills rolling away into the distance, impressive sights that caught and held his eye, much as they did the eye of many a Barbizon painter. With John Sell Cotman (1782-1842), a pupil of Crome, we have landscapes revealing a more intimate communion of the artist and nature. Cotman, moreover, followed his master in standing out against the historical landscape, whether allegorical or mythological. He was fond of large masses, which he treated with depth and fullness; his light is more than mere 'lighting' and some of his pictures have been compared to Corot's. Thus we see English landscape-painting acquiring an international character, whose new directions were to have memorable effects on future art.

CONSTABLE'S IMPRESSIONISM

It was with Constable and Turner that English landscape-painting came into its own, and thanks to them that the landscape won its independence as a self-sufficient form of art. Firstly because it gave full expression to the affinities between the artist and nature; then because it led to the creation of a new technique appropriate to it; and lastly because it called for specific procedures which throughout the 19th century were to conflict with academic tradition. Thus Constable ridiculed the academic painters who made their pictures out of other pictures and plaster-casts and knew "as little of nature as a hackney-coach horse does of a pasture."

In such scathing terms did he indict the painting of his day. Yet, judging by his self-portrait, John Constable (1776-1837) was a quiet, mild young man with a sentimental turn of mind and large eyes that looked wonderingly on the world. He was engaged to a girl for sixteen years before marrying her. He remained in England in 'splendid isolation' and knew little more of the world than his birthplace and its environs. He made a short stay in Paris, went there a second time, and that was all, although it has been said that Paris launched his fame. Never did he make the trip to Italy, the land elected by so many artists for their honeymoon with painting.

The truth is that his observant eye needed no wider horizon than that of a wheat-field, a meadow, trees, a brook. Air and light were the breath of life to him, and the life of his art, too. He painted the countryside as he would have tilled the soil, had he been a farmer and not a plain country gentleman whom his family wanted to become a clergyman. Constable is credited with being the first painter to set up his easel in the open country. His love of nature was neither eclectic, literary nor historical. Instinctively he penetrated to the sources of her being and saw with his mind's eye the rising of the sap that quickens her. Stirred to a rapture already half way to romanticism, he could be realistic on occasion, as when he ridiculed the connoisseurs who set up "black, rubbed out, and dirty canvases" against God's works. He was already seeing reality with the eye of an Impressionist when he said that no two days or hours are alike, "neither were there ever two leaves of a tree alike since the creation of the world." A remark of Chateaubriand, in his *Lettre sur le paysage* (1795), had found its echo: "The same motif seen in a different light takes on another aspect, a different emotional expression."

Constable's whole artistic outlook is conveyed in the opinions we have quoted. While conscious of a deep communion with nature, he also felt that somehow he must record the all-pervading mobility he sensed in her. He was ever sadly conscious of the tyranny of time, and in his art he sought to give the fleeting moment immortality. Such was the temperament which enabled Constable to bring a landscape to life, and to invent a new technique for an aesthetic which was to give one of the forms of romanticism a place in art.

An artist whose aim is to express his emotions never subjects himself to the directives of any other artists, even the greatest. It was this first move towards freedom that was the beginning of Romanticism. Cézanne called himself a "primitive," and the same might have been said of Constable. He, too, never troubled about setting up a system, but confined himself to expressing his personal feelings to the utmost, without tampering with them. Unlike Delacroix, he was no visionary; history and religion had no interest for him, nor had myths or legends, however human their appeal. His art is one long hymn of praise to nature, whether he is depicting her under her grandiose aspects or, in gentler accents, responding to her quieter, more intimate charms. Nature for Delacroix was but a "dictionary" which he consulted in the making of a picture;

JOHN CONSTABLE (1776-1837). WEYMOUTH BAY, C. 1819. (21 × 29 ½″) REPRODUCED BY COURTESY OF THE TRUSTEES, THE NATIONAL GALLERY, LONDON.

When they set out to break free from the traditional 'historical landscape' of Poussin and Claude Lorrain, it was to nature, much more than to the Dutch landscapists, that the English painters John Crome and Constable turned at the beginning of the 19th century. Thus Constable anticipated such French landscape-painters as Courbet, Boudin and Claude Monet. Here, with a vision romantic through and through, Constable was inspired to a marvelous rendering of sky, clouds, waves and cliffs. He does not go out for the 'picturesque,' or linger over details. This work throbs with the very pulse of nature, whose grandeur was the constant object of the artist's admiration.

1914

Here Constable proves himself a real precursor, in his desire to capture the impression produced on him by an effect of atmosphere, for rendering which he utilizes his palette of intense blues and glazes, his sure, free style and vibrant hatchings. We can understand why Delacroix was so greatly impressed by his fresh and original conception of how a landscape should be treated. Constable never 'arranged' a scene, but in true painterly fashion probed into the elements composing it. Already impressionist in his realist observation of nature, he heaped scorn on the "brown trees," the "black... and dirty canvases" then ranking as high art.

for Constable she was the sole source of his creative impulse. His outlook on nature is full of religious feeling, whereas that of Delacroix is frankly pagan. Constable's very technique is a part of himself, at the service of his feelings rather than at that of any ideal concept. When he lit on new methods of expression such as the breaking up of tones into a host of variants, this was not because he had any special interest in technical adventures, but because these procedures enabled him the better to do homage to the object of his love and to extol its beauty. The grandeur we find in so much of his work is never spectacular, because he never deliberately aimed at it. We have an impression that he let the inspiration of the moment—whose source he neither knew nor sought to know—direct his brush. Thus it is that Constable's compositions never show the framework upon which they are built. Nor does he aim at panoramic effects or selected 'angles of vision.' In fact he anticipated Courbet's advice about setting up one's easel anywhere, no matter where, and going ahead. The fact that he set it up at a given spot merely authenticated the emotion to which the scene gave rise. It was not his way to 'arrange' the landscape; there was nothing conventional or mannered in his art. And if in *Weymouth Bay* (see Plate) we notice how he stresses the three successive pair of parallels—the two diagonals in the cloud-groups, those of the hill and the stones in the foreground, and, lastly, the two curves made by the waterline on the foreshore and by the slope of the cliff on the right—we must admit that this is the prying eye of the art critic at work, for so simple and fluid are these rhythms that their presence is felt rather than noticed by the normal observer. We might almost say the difference is like that between free verse and alexandrines. *Salisbury Cathedral* (see Plate) is another illustration of Constable's intuitive, natural craftsmanship. Never would any classical landscapist have risked placing that pointed tree on the left of the steeple, and masking it, or the huge oak on its right so dramatically 'crushing' it. Indeed this lay-out, with its juxtaposition of objects following no predetermined plan, is exactly that of the Primitives. In any case the picturesqueness cherished by his English predecessors had no appeal for Constable.

Naturally enough, Constable's novel approach had a far from favorable reception. His work was called "chaotic" and Ruskin sharply criticized it at first. Constable had to wait until the 1824 Paris Salon for his triumph, and belated recognition in his own country. Bonington and several other English painters exhibited at the 1824 Salon, and their works were a revelation. After seeing one of Constable's pictures, Delacroix retouched the sky in his *Massacres de Scio* and was later heard to say: "That fellow Constable has done me a world of good." His name was soon on the lips of everyone of consequence in the art and literary worlds and his pictures were welcomed for their freshness and vitality. That *Corn Field* (painted at noon, he tells us, "under a pleasant and healthful breeze") gave a new direction to the art of landscape painting. All the more so as his conceptions were implemented by a broad, sumptuous technique that swept all before it. He did not apply color with the bland uniformity of the academic painters, but used it in a new spirit, breaking down the same tone into an endless variety of nuances. Casting idealism by the board, he sought only for the true, since, as he said, "nothing in nature is ugly." A remark which justified the admiration and friendly rivalry of such men as Delacroix, Courbet and Millet. And here we have the beginnings of the influence, so diverse in its manifestations, that Constable's art had on his successors.

THE MAGIC OF TURNER

William Turner's temperament was on a different scale altogether. He, too, was a landscape-painter, but above all a visionary, inspired by a profoundly mystical outlook on nature. He was a thorough-going romantic in the sense that his introvert personality was steeped in poetic emotion, and to this was due the tendency we find in that portion

J. M. W. TURNER (1775-1851). RAIN, STEAM AND SPEED. (36 × 48″) REPRODUCED BY COURTESY OF THE TRUSTEES, THE NATIONAL GALLERY, LONDON.

This picture, painted with extraordinary freedom, marks the climax of a long career of unflagging research. After beginning as an architectural draftsman, Turner studied the work of Claude Lorrain and the Dutch Masters. He was in the habit of using watercolors for jotting down his impressions while traveling, and this led him to adopt a palette of intense colors in his oil paintings, so as to match the vivid tones of the watercolors.

of his output which is at once most characteristic and was the most severely criticized: a passionate addiction for, as it were, intoxicating himself with color such as had never been seen before in painting.

"I have never done but one portrait," Turner once said. And this was his own, in which the eyes are those of a man rapt in a sort of ecstasy. He was the only son of a humble London barber. After having seen his mother lose her mind and die while he was yet a boy—a fact often alluded to by those who stress heredity—Turner cherished a warm affection for his father, a rather odd person by all accounts. He never left his father's side, however, and the latter, too, was devoted to his son, often defending his interests in a rather grotesque manner. Psychoanalysts doubtless might find in this curious "father-fixation" a subject after their own hearts. Crossed in love, Turner never married and seems to have had no love-life. Something of an invalid, he was neither cheerful nor companionable, even in his youth. As a small boy, he often slipped out of his father's shop and roamed the banks of the Thames, where he came to love the water, the fogs, the barges and the sea-going ships, which he soon took to sketching. His father exhibited some of the lad's drawings in his shop and customers began to buy them. Both father and son were, moreover, rather grasping in money matters. At the age of fifteen Turner exhibited at the Royal Academy. Reynolds encouraged him and his reputation quickly grew. He was only twenty-seven when he was appointed teacher of perspective at the Royal Academy. He traveled abroad, to France, Switzerland, Germany, Italy. All this time his life ran a smooth course and he was tirelessly at work. A comfortable income requited his efforts and satisfied his cupidity. Thus his life passed until, when he was fifty, the shattering blow came from which he never recovered: his father's death. Urged by his friends to travel, he did so, but got little joy of it. He went back to Italy, visited Venice for the first time, was dazzled and enraptured by what he saw. There he continued working; but once back in England he found the loneliness of home without his father more than he could bear. Unable to settle down again, he began to lead a nomadic existence, took to drinking, spent his days in and out of taverns and was often missing for weeks on end. His work became sporadic and now developed a new mode of expression, eerie and disconcerting. Faithful to the end, an aged housekeeper, who had served Turner and his father many years, spent most of her time trying to trace his whereabouts. One winter morning she found him registered under an assumed name in a shabby inn—but death had preceded her by a few hours. By the terms of his will, the greater part of his considerable fortune went to the founding of a home for sick and aged artists.

Turner's art developed its most characteristic features after his father's death and his visit to Venice. The latter event seems to have fired his imagination. Drunk with air, light and color, he inhabited an enchanted world of his own making, in which he wandered, void of thoughts. The subjects of his pictures grew more and more evanescent, lost in a haze of shimmering color. The fulfilment, in terms of painting, of Novalis' wish: "If only one could write with no particular subject in mind!" Turner now began appending short, unintelligible poems to his pictures. His work became an art of shreds and patches, pure color symphonies: incredible skies, drifting mists, fogs, and clouds. Formerly so devoted to Claude and to the Dutch masters, he now cast all restraint to the winds. Yet he had painted such splendidly constructed pictures as *Dido and Aeneas* and *Apollo and the Sibyl* and his moving *Death of Nelson*, with its exciting but nobly balanced upswing of masts, sails and clouds. In this last phase his art became—like Monet's in his later years—a sheer phantasmagoria of pure, abstract color. Put on with a "drunken broom" was a famous comment on Courbet's color, but it would better apply to Turner. Wholly free of literary allusions, his romanticism was of a purely pictorial order, and bore fruit in a technique of quite new procedures, such as the tinting of shadows in blue or red, an innovation which was not lost on the Impressionists and their followers.

The art of Turner's last phase was one of pure, untrammelled instinct; exuberant, spontaneous, devoid of any artifice or affectation. But we cannot leave his mother's insanity out of account, nor deny that these rapturous emotions stemmed from a mind incapable of that self-control and sense of due measure, hall-marks of all true craftsmanship in art, which are so conspicuously lacking in the more characteristic part of his art, whose heroic stature, nevertheless, is not to be denied.

BONINGTON

A newcomer from England, Richard Bonington was already a regular visitor at the Louvre at the age of fifteen. Delacroix, little older himself, had met him there and been much impressed by his venturesome yet well-balanced temperament. A pupil of Gros, the young Englishman endorsed his master's mild disapproval of David's teachings, as well as his lyrical propensities and his zest for color. "One can never have too much air and space," he often said. French scenery delighted him, though it was in watercolor, that typically English medium, that he best interpreted his delicate responses to natural beauty, with a matchless grace and lightness of touch. On canvas he sometimes fell short of the full expression his romantic fancy clamored for. But his seascapes provide convincing proof of his innate sense of the grandiose; of almost epic proportions, his skies often take up three-fourths of the canvas and convey an impression of boundless space like that which Tiepolo had conjured up in his cupolas.

Bonington died at the age of twenty-six. We may

R. P. BONINGTON (1801-1828). THE NORMANDY COAST. (17 ½ × 15″) LOUVRE, PARIS.

Delacroix said Bonington's works were like jewels "that flatter and delight the eye, independently of any subject, and apart from any nature-imitation." Coming from a master who neglected neither of these aspects of art, this remark is of much interest, and it emphasizes the very human romanticism of the young painter.

well ask ourselves if his feverish enthusiasm could have withstood the test of a longer life, and whether he had not said all he had to say. For so faultless is his technique that one wonders if he could have carried his art any farther.

Although Bonington's contribution to the Romantic movement was a very valuable one, it must be admitted that his temperament brought to it nothing absolutely new or comparable with the work of his great compeers; nothing to suggest that his work was to have any far-reaching influence on a century that brought so many upheavals in the world of art.

The youthful imagination of the artist was still groping among a variety of 'genres' for its most congenial form of expression. It is in the landscape that Bonington seems at last to have found himself. Even here, however, he continued to experiment with different procedures. At the start of his brief career he had done a number of large seascapes in watercolor or sepia, full of light and air, depicting the Normandy coast and the banks of the Seine. At that time he tended to lay in his pigment over-copiously, rather clumsily, like so many quite young painters who feel they have much to say, but have not yet learned to say it simply. It was only later that he adopted those light, marvelously translucent touches, glowing through their luminous scumble, that are so much more convincing than the lavish impasto of his earlier phase. After having yielded to the lures of color, always so dangerous to the young painter, he gave thought to the structure of the composition. He visited Italy, studied Corot, painted monuments, churches, streets and squares, among them his famous *Place du Molard* (at Geneva). Most impressive in these are his powerful, condensed effects of light and shadow. When, on occasion, he turned to subjects calling for the human figure he gave little thought to realistic likeness. Amongst his figure studies are *An Odalisque*, with its echoes of Lawrence's grace and elegance, and his *Woman at her Easel*, in which he tries his hand at painting an interior, with Vermeer obviously in mind.

In short it would seem that Bonington, throughout his brief career, kept open house to a great variety of influences.

WORKS OF THE ENGLISH LANDSCAPISTS
EXHIBITED AT THE 1824 SALON

(In view of its documentary interest, we reproduce the following extract exactly as it appeared in the official catalogue of the 1824 Paris Salon.)

BONINGTON

Etude en Flandre. — Marine. — Vue d'Abbeville, aquarelle. — Marine (des pêcheurs débarquant leurs poissons). — Une plage sablonneuse.

CONSTABLE

Une charrette à foin traversant un gué au pied d'une ferme, paysage. — Un canal en Angleterre, paysage (on voit sur le premier plan des barques et des personnages). — Vue près de Londres, Hampstead-Heath.

COPLEY FIELDING

Vue de Hastings, sur les côtes de Sussex. — Vue de Hythe et des marais de Romney. — Vue sur la Tamise, à Deptford, près de Londres. — Vue d'après nature en Angleterre, aquarelle. — Une petite marine, id. — Vue du château de Chepstow, id. — Vue du château d'Harlech, id. — Route dans une plaine, id. — Pleine mer avec embarcation, id.

THALES FIELDING

Macbeth rencontrant les sorcières sur la bruyère, aquarelle. — Moulin près la barrière d'Italie. — Un cadre contenant des aquarelles.

HARDING

Vue d'Aysgarth, dans le comté d'York.

JAMES ROBERTS

Vue de Rouen avant l'incendie de 1822, aquarelle. — Vue de Beauvais, id.

JOHN VARLEY

Montagne de Morne, en Irlande. — Une composition.

WILD

Vue prise de l'intérieur de la cathédrale d'Amiens. — Nef de la cathédrale de Reims. — Vue prise dans l'intérieur de l'église Saint-Ouen, à Rouen. — Portail du midi de la cathédrale de Chartres.

The Salon of 1824, with its showing of English painters, opened the way to Impressionism. Sixty years later, in 1884, the first Salon des Indépendants opened in Paris, at which Signac, Seurat and Odilon Redon were the most remarkable representatives. There the Impressionist experiment was brought to a close. To the analytical procedures which ended in the dissolution of forms new attempts at building form succeeded, and modern painting was in the offing.

3
COLOR AND THE CREATIVE SPIRIT
NATURE AND FORMS

GÉRICAULT · DELACROIX · DAUMIER
MILLET · COURBET

*A*FTER *the French Revolution, man's personal right to free expression was undisputed, and taste for factual truth held sway. The romantic painters—Gros, Géricault, Delacroix—scrutinized with keen attention the real life around them and dreamed of recording in paint the great events of their time. But, carried away by poetic emotion, Delacroix was soon wholly wrapped up in his dreams and the fantasies of his imagination, that 'queen of faculties,' thanks to which he could plunge himself back into earlier ages, body forth visions from the great books of the world, and steep his mind in the magical enchantments of the East. Daumier had a gift of expression none the less effective for taking its rise from the men and women he saw around him, and whose portrayals he raised to a level of timeless authenticity. However in these men, as in the case of Millet and Courbet, contemporaries saw only triviality, immorality, the total lack of an ideal. To them it seemed unthinkable that these painters could serve a lofty ambition, in itself an ideal of a kind: that of adhering to the truth, an earthly, flesh-and-blood truth, and thereby furthering painting as an art by extending the range of its subject-matter. This 'realism' was to exercise a considerable influence on all modern painting, for it ushered in not only a period of 'expressionist' inquiry into human character, but also an era of exhaustive analysis of the very stuff of painting, an analysis resembling chemical research, so eager were painters to discover, down to the last details, all the resources of their craft.*

GÉRICAULT

Antoine Gros (1771-1835) is sometimes looked upon as a French precursor of Romanticism. Yet his art is essentially classical, despite the fine poetic feeling of his color, and it was not for nothing that David left him in charge of his pupils when he went into exile. Gros it was, too, who one day said to Thomas Couture, that indifferent painter: "Ah, Couture, if only you were older, we could smash these upstart romantics." Some say it was in despair at being regarded as a romantic himself that Gros killed himself at the age of sixty-four.

The romantic movement in French painting would seem actually to have been launched on its career by Géricault when at the 1812 Salon, to the horrified dismay of the established critics and masters, he exhibited his famous *Officier de la garde impériale chargeant*. The twenty-year-old artist had just painted the work in twelve days' time, and its disorderly magnificence and boldness revealed a startling precocity.

Géricault was a blond, good-looking youth, well-dressed, full of charm, enamored of fame and the pleasures of life, and for ever spending more than he earned. Yet he was a man of orderly habits, even meticulous, and went so far as to number his pictures and drawings, down to the smallest sketches. He was dreamy, given to melancholy, and endured like Constable and Turner the pangs of disappointed love; indeed he once said in a letter to a friend: "If there's one thing sure in life, it's that we're born to suffer." To the very sincere sorrow of all who knew him, he died of tuberculosis at thirty-three, an age destined to prove fatal to several 19th-century masters.

Géricault's sketches are not above the ordinary. No intellectual, he liked to spend his time in stables, either making sketches of horses or perfecting his horsemanship. His two loves were Rubens—and the well-known rider Franconi. As a young man, he made the time-honored trip to Italy. Here an interesting question suggests itself: what do artists make of this classic encounter, and what do they bring back from it? Géricault admitted that he "trembled before the masters," that he momentarily lost faith in himself and took some time to regain his confidence. He regained it the more easily as his inspiration always sprang from the depths of his being and never from the works of other artists. Though, like most painters, he made copies of others' works, he always interpreted them in the light of his own feelings. He was fond of contrasts of light and shade, and Guérin, that insipid painter, once said to him: "Really, your contrasts make one think you always paint by moonlight." He put on color grandly, always preferring values to tones. Also he liked feats of virtuosity, and when a model posed with her right arm raised, he would sketch her in the opposite attitude. His romantic *brio* is well conveyed by his remark: "I start a sketch of a woman, and it comes out a lion!" Actually he hardly needed a model. His way was not to copy reality, but to transfigure it, and lift it to quite amazing heights, to the vast bewilderment of his fellow-painters. Delacroix once said of him: "He improves on everything he touches, and gives new life to it." A very authentic, realistic life, we might add. The secret of Géricault's dynamic art is to be found in his love of nature, and perhaps also in his love of the horse, which he regarded as an incarnation of the life-force. This habit of identifying himself with objects that matched his tempestuous imagination came to him so instinctively that his art is a language of living signs, reminding us of the amazing feats of the prehistoric animal-painters.

THÉODORE GÉRICAULT (1791-1824). HORSE HELD BY SLAVES, C. 1817. (18½ × 23")
MUSÉE DES BEAUX-ARTS, ROUEN.

Whether treating a contemporary news event like the wreck of the frigate *La Méduse*, or a scene like the street horse-race he saw at Rome in 1816, and which inspired this picture, Géricault strips away all non-essentials and imparts a real grandeur and style to the subject. In this vigorous study for a large-scale picture which he planned to paint, we may note his fondness for full-bodied, sculptural volumes and for violent contrasts of light and shade, which bring out his kinship with Daumier.

DELACROIX AND HIS WORLD

History has conferred on Delacroix the honor of being the head of the Romantic School. But would the master himself have appreciated this honor? Almost certainly he would not, for his imagination, vivid as it was, seems always to have been controlled by his intellect and he never faltered in his loyalty to the great classical painters, for whom—unlike Courbet—he showed the warmest admiration. Moreover Delacroix explicitly denied any romantic bias; the day came when he even disowned his early enthusiasm for Shakespeare and Goethe. He was always drawing attention to his preparatory drawings and sketches, so as to rebut the charges of facility and improvisation so often leveled at him. In repudiating the epithet 'romantic,' Delacroix was probably giving expression to a harmless foible of many great artists—their distaste for being assigned to any particular school, when they would prefer to have emphasis laid on their personality as individuals. For, as we shall see, Delacroix possessed all the traits which go to make the true romantic, or, at any rate, which fit in with our conception of that Byronic personality.

To begin with, he had the outward aspect of the typical romantic as we picture him; he was tall and slender, with jet-black hair, glowing eyes, a gaunt face with high cheek-bones, a dark complexion described as 'Mexican' by some who knew him, and the air of a Hamlet constantly buffeted by a "sea of troubles." Also he was, by nature, morbid, passionate, ever ready to take offence, and blessed, or cursed, with an egotism that led him to stress his individuality to the utmost. In the expression of his individualism, however, he very often exercised a salutary restraint, due no doubt to an acute intelligence ever quick to curb the vagaries of the instinct. It should, perhaps, be mentioned that his early years were marked by a remarkable series of near-fatal accidents: as a baby he narrowly missed being burnt alive; as a youngster he almost died of verdigris poisoning, was all but choked to death by a bunch of grapes, nearly got strangled by a sabretache belt, and he was once fished out of Marseilles harbor in a half-drowned state. It is said that he was an illegitimate son of Talleyrand, in which case the hereditary influence of that aristocratic republican, physically unsound but gifted with an intellect of the highest order, might account for many of his peculiarities. He was given a sound education at the Lycée Louis-le-Grand in Paris and was, as David and Ingres had been, a devotee of music before turning his hand to painting, at which he got off to a bad start, meeting with no success in the competitions at the Ecole des Beaux-Arts and getting little encouragement from his first master, that rather mawkish painter Guérin. This only served to exasperate a temperament irritable enough to start with, and now, as was only natural, he sought to exteriorize his rancor by painting violent and tragic scenes: storm-laden skies, battles, massacres, shipwrecks and fires, all appropriately crowded with hapless captives, children trampled by runaway horses, sprawling corpses, slaughtered beasts, convulsionaries and so forth. He treated these spectacular happenings on suitably dramatic lines: excited linework,

1918

huge masses, vivid, violently contrasting colors which he broke down into an exhaustive range of nuances.

In carrying out such a program, how could he hope to get the better of his temperamental restlessness and waywardness? He totally lacked the rigid, inflexible integrity of such men as David, Ingres or Courbet. His concern seems to have been to stand up for himself rather than for his art. "I make my pictures more for myself than

1919

EUGÈNE DELACROIX (1798-1863). ST GEORGE AND THE DRAGON, 1847. (11×14″) LOUVRE, PARIS.

In painting this small picture Delacroix used vibrant, translucent touches put on with watercolor brushes; hence the remarkable brilliance and the richness of the hues. After doing a number of sketches of the animals in the Jardin des Plantes, he was able to build up an extraordinarily convincing dragon reminding us of the finest dragons in Chinese art and without the slightest resemblance to the pasteboard monster Ingres shows us in his *Roger delivering Angelica*. Delacroix' rendering of the dragon answers to his special taste for the stuff of poetry and fable, a taste so pronounced that under his brush the monster takes on quite imposing proportions.

for the public," he said. And again: "Watteau and Rubens are too artistic,... I thrive on the upsurge of my own feelings." So keen a champion of his Ego, a man so enamored of color, movement and historical scenes, is surely to be reckoned an adept of romanticism, along the lines of one of the two tendencies mentioned above. In another age he would have had to hide his hypersensitivity from others, but thanks to the new spirit of freedom prevailing in France, he was able to give free rein to his temperament. For that matter, was not this championship of his Ego inbred rather than romantic? We must remember that he was a bachelor of the 'fussy' type, jealous of his privacy, and he knew only too well that his restlessness was an outcome of his constitution. It would be true to say that he stood in dread of his Ego, and was always in quest of

EUGÈNE DELACROIX (1798-1863). THE TIGER HUNT, 1854. (29 × 36½") LOUVRE, PARIS.

Here we have Delacroix' dynamic temperament finding full expression in a maelstrom of vivid color. Irresistibly the powerful arabesques rise and fall, swell and spread, leap up and swirl in circular rhythms round the hunter's lance—which, the one straight line in the picture, plays the part of the conductor's baton in this glittering symphony of movement. "Straight lines are monsters," Delacroix once remarked—and the great artist has successfully tamed the "monster" in this picture: the Arab's lance.

1920

EUGÈNE DELACROIX (1798-1863). THE CHESS-PLAYERS. (15 ½ × 27 ½")
WILDENSTEIN GALLERY, NEW YORK.

This picture is undated. In the catalogue of the Delacroix Exhibition at the Louvre in 1950 it was grouped with a number of works dated 1834. A close examination of its construction and tonalities, however, may lead us to feel some doubt as to this dating; the oriental theme of the work, though found in many pictures of that period, is not enough to warrant it, for we find such themes recurring in Delacroix' later years. As a matter of fact, it seems more probable that he painted this picture during the last decade of his life, for in it he achieves that synthesis between the untrammelled imagination and classical discipline to which he constantly aspired. The dynamic expression of *The Tiger Hunt* has given way to static qualities, imparting a monumental style to the work. Here Delacroix is no longer a composer of huge, tumultuous symphonies but a discreet harmonist of colors which, no longer clashing and striking out sparks, merge in deep, untroubled union.

'escape' from his predicament, but escape in a form congenial to his health and orderly habits. Thus he found solace, not like Baudelaire, in drug-taking, but in painting, traveling and social life. Art, for him, was a psychical 'transfer.' Hence his taste for air, light and free movement, so pronounced indeed that, all things considered, he preferred at heart the luminous fragrance of the English landscape to the hot-house atmosphere of the Venetians. This preference is the more interesting in that it indicates the form Delacroix' romanticism tended to take. His precarious health, the dangerous accidents of his early years, his faltering start as a young painter, his hypochondria, irritability and constant restlessness, all contributed to put him on his guard against his own sensibility, from which he seems to have felt that nothing good could come. He was too skeptical, too logically minded, to be a prey to conceit and self-love, as was the case with Courbet. Nor did he harbor the least illusion about his own attitude to nature, which was for him, as he himself declared, no more than a "dictionary," in other words, an implement, a stand-by, a means and not an end. His romanticism was not keyed to the sentimental mood of Constable's, though it was perhaps with a hint of regret he sighed: "That fellow Constable has done me a world of good!"

No doubt he welcomed any relief from an excitability of which he must have been all too painfully aware when he contemplated the serenity of the English landscapists. But his temperament denied him their happy understanding of the life of nature. His instinctive distaste for any sort of introspection led him to a wholly objective approach to art; hence his fondness for 'dynamic' subjects, whose turbulent vitality gave scope for his personal ideas regarding the use of color. Of this there is no better example than his *Tiger Hunt* (see Plate), which dynamically sums up his form of Romanticism. True, and we noted it at the start, Delacroix balked at being assigned to the Romantic School. And his objections were honest ones, for he continually strove to bring his work into line with that of the classical masters, and shared to the full their respect of correct, orderly procedure.

We can learn much of the problems Delacroix set himself, and never satisfactorily solved, from his fascinating *Journal*. Though he boldly wrote that "the artist need not bother about sticking to his resolutions," he was always trying to abide by his. This illustrates one facet of his genius; and it tends to explain the contrast between the solid virtues of his admirable *Jewish Wedding* and the turbulent *Barque of Dante*. Feeling the need to bridle his dramatic imagination, Delacroix tried to sublimate his emotive drives to a pitch of genuine force and truthfulness, by harmonizing all the forms of his sensibility. In other words, by idealizing his own personality. Thus the old desire for classical construction lingered on in him, and we cannot assign Delacroix to that band of 'admirable savages' of whom Courbet may be regarded as the precursor and several 19th-century artists as illustrious examples. His keen intellect kept him from any crude display of feeling. He loathed displays of mere artistry and it is well known how he exclaimed at seeing a seascape by Ruisdael that it "reached the summit of art because the art in it was completely hidden from view." If Delacroix aspired to carry his methods to perfection, this was never with an eye to mere technical finish, but rather so as to impart the greatest possible intensity and harmony to the picture. It was, moreover, due to his distaste for the 'set piece' and the 'bravura passage' that his observant eye led him on to the division of tones, the interplay of complementaries, constructive color all but blotting out the drawing, contrasting, juxtaposed touches, and a rendering of the vibrations of atmospheric light. Though he was not the discoverer of these procedures, he was the first to exploit them systematically and carry them to a hitherto undreamt-of pitch of harmonious intensity. The man Delacroix always held the artist in check, whereas with Courbet the artist enjoyed unbridled freedom. Thus it was that Delacroix never permitted himself those vagaries in which color sinks to the merest patchwork. He initiated a new technique precisely because he never 'let his brush run away with him.' Thus, ever on his guard, he kept in wise control that very romanticism of which he himself, in so inspired a way, is one of the most exemplary practitioners. He is a master in the highest sense of the word, that connoting absolute mastery of the medium; hence the influence of a life's work which still holds its own today, as much by the noble example it provides as by its sheer painterly effectiveness.

HUMANITY OF DAUMIER

Unkindly though his period may have served him, history is not to blame if Daumier became a realist. Nor was it merely for aesthetic reasons that he devoted himself to probing human feelings, nor a purely moral bias that led him, in his lithographs, to vent his hatred of injustice, crime and human folly. And, finally, if he evolved a highly personal style and a color-scheme at once sober and emotive, this was not the outcome of methods he deliberately chose or took from others. The truth is that realism was both a second nature with him and the consequence of the life he led. Actually, however, he never set up as an adept of realism, indeed it never occurred to him to apply the term to his art; still less to repudiate it, as Courbet did—after proclaiming to all the world the unique merits of the realist approach.

From an artist who all his life was harassed by ill luck and poverty, we can hardly expect a show of happy enthusiasm for the ways of men and the look of things. The lot of Ingres, Delacroix, Corot and Courbet, for example, was a relatively favorable one; Daumier, however (whose fame began after his death), was born poor, lived on a mere pittance and died nearly blind and almost penniless, without even the consolation that his genius had been given its due. Why then should he have been moved to view this vale of tears as the best of all possible worlds, or to paint it in rosy colors? It was, on the contrary, only natural that he should seek measures of defense against the hard knocks that came his way, this "world he never made." It was natural, too, perhaps, that he thought to see the root of his troubles in a badly constituted social order. Thus, instead of the pure inventor of forms he would have liked to be, he developed into a shrewd observer whose eye found endless matter for satire. Thus he remained until he found some relief from a jaundiced attitude for which we can hardly blame him—that is to say, until his circumstances improved a little, at least judged by his standards, which were not exacting. So he came finally to adopt a stoic outlook, to take the frailties of human nature as he found them and, quietly observant, to create types of humanity whose verisimilitude moves us no less than their grandeur.

This, in brief, was how life served Daumier, that sensitive, simple-hearted artist of whom Balzac once said: "Friend Daumier has Michelangelo's blood in his veins."

Honoré Daumier was born at Marseilles; his mother came from the same city, and his father, also from the south, was a glass-maker, something of a poet, and a would-be reformer in the manner of Jean-Jacques Rousseau. He was a great talker, a bohemian, and inclined to be ambitious. When the boy was seven, the family migrated to Paris, where they lived in extreme poverty. At fifteen, Daumier became junior clerk in a process-server's office, where he had his initiation into the mysteries of business and pettifoggery. An extremely wide-awake, if ingenuous, lad, he missed nothing of what was going on around him. Next, he was employed in a bookstore and struck up acquaintance with a few artists. From now on, he began to sketch, took a keen interest in lithography and published a few of his efforts in *La Silhouette*, a fashion periodical.

HONORÉ DAUMIER (1808-1879).
THE WASHERWOMAN. (19½ × 13″)
LOUVRE, PARIS

From a small window in his studio Daumier had a view of the Quai des Célestins on the Seine. Thus he became familiar with the varied spectacle of sailors, dockhands at work, horses, dogs and children bathing or frolicking on the banks, women scrubbing clothes at the water's edge. This sober, powerfully conceived work, with its solid, monumental lay-out, is filled with a warm sense of the human, making it a moving page from everyday life and an example of Daumier's realism.

Soon after he was taken on the staff of *Charivari*, a political paper. There he met Balzac, who gave him a piece of true Balzacian advice: "If you want to get on in life, my boy, *make debts!*" But this he could never bring himself to do. Timid and easily swayed, he was, as might be expected, a pawn in the hands of the political hot-heads working on *Charivari*. And finally, when his *Gargantua* appeared, a lithograph showing King Louis-Philippe swallowing civil-lists and disgorging posts and decorations, he paid for it with a short spell of jail. He was then twenty-six, and the exploit promptly brought him into the limelight; the financial advantages of this publicity were slight, still now he was able to help out his parents a little. He went ahead as a caricaturist, deputies, judges, the military, officials and the like being his favorite butts. On the side he made sculptures, small busts in a grotesque style representing such well-known contemporaries as Thiers, Guizot, and Doctor Prunelle. These were never spiteful, but always vivid and droll. On one occasion, however, Daumier did lose his temper: this was over the 'Rue Transnonain' shootings, and his picture of this scene has become famous, such is its technical perfection and its grim ferocity. Meanwhile he married, and this new responsibility did not make things easier, for the market for his particular kind of painting was almost non-existent. All the more so as he was an ardent republican, and thus it was not to him that well-to-do buyers came.

HONORÉ DAUMIER (1808-1879). THE REVOLT, C. 1848. (30 ½ × 16″) THE PHILLIPS COLLECTION, WASHINGTON.

For this picture, remarkable for the boldness of the drawing, it would seem that Daumier drew on what he had actually seen of the riots and street-fighting that broke out in Paris between the fall of Louis-Philippe and the *coup d'État* of 1851. It is in works of this kind that we see most clearly that, even if he chose his subjects from the everyday life of his time, Daumier handled them in a thoroughly romantic way. Giving no heed to the myriad details of reality, he took from the scene just those essential forms that suited his purpose.

1848-9

HONORÉ DAUMIER (1808-1879). THE REFUGEES. (6×11″) PALAIS DES BEAUX-ARTS DE LA VILLE, PARIS.

There exist several versions—paintings and drawings—of this theme, which Daumier also treated in a bas-relief. Some have thought that he was evoking Lamennais' description of the "hapless exile"; others, that he had in mind the Polish refugees from Czarist despotism. In any case, he did not trouble to give any particular setting to the unhappy group; they are of no time or country. Daumier has confined himself to a poignant yet superbly grandiose expression of his sympathy with those who are forced to flee their native country.

Daumier's lithographs reveal the rebel he was at heart; but, as we have said, his outbursts were never malevolent. Though he showed the faces and the ways of his fellow-men as they really were, he did so without malice, and always with a smile in reserve. He directed his satire not only on the more glaring vices, but on mere human foibles, too, and with unfailing wit. Thus it was that he represented Monsieur Prud'homme, the average bourgeois, in company with a flower-crowned skeleton, blowing on a kind of double horn—this he called "Peace, an Idyll." Forain once said of him: "Ah, Daumier! He was different; his heart was in the right place."

His lithographs bring out his amazing gift of draftsmanship. The linework is neat, assured, accurate, vigorously hatched; contrasts are neatly balanced against each other. Daumier also had that rare talent of being able to draw and paint entirely from memory, without the aid of models.

Yet the great Daumier, the real genius, was not the lithographer, but the painter; though as such he remained unknown in his lifetime and for many years after his death.

While earning his living as a caricaturist, he found time to visit the Louvre regularly and copied the masters, both painters and sculptors, especially the latter; the effect of this is visible both in the modeling of his figures and in his own sculptures, one of which, *The Refugees*, is nothing short of superb. He was on friendly terms with the great artists of his time, Décamps, Ruet, Millet, Rousseau, Préault, Corot and Delacroix. The latter studied and made copies of a number of his

drawings; while Baudelaire called him "one of our leading men, not only in caricature, but in modern art." The historian Michelet, one of his closest friends, wrote to him: "We have plenty of agreeable artists, but you alone have real driving force." Differing from the general public, artists prefer Daumier the painter, to Daumier the lithographer. They are impressed by two qualities which in themselves sum up Daumier's genius: his humanity and his poetic sense, both of which correspond to the ideal contemporary painting sets before itself. For Daumier's art always gave expression

HONORÉ DAUMIER (1808-1879). DON QUIXOTE AND SANCHO PANZA. (15 ½ × 12 ½") RICHARD C. PAINE COLLECTION, BOSTON.

Molière's plays, and Cervantes' *Don Quixote* were the literary works which above all fired Daumier's artistic imagination. In the generous enthusiasm and idealism of Don Quixote and the earthy common sense and prudence of Sancho Panza, he doubtless saw a reflection of his own dual nature. Though he never actually went to Spain, Daumier's lifelong predilection for vast, barren spaces enabled him to evoke a convincing picture of the wild, rocky regions of the Iberian peninsula.

to his natural warmth of heart, as we see in his paintings of schoolchildren coming home from school, or bathing in the Seine, or the parents of a drowned child carrying away the little body. With unfailing sympathy for the human situation, he depicted washerwomen, melancholy acrobats, street musicians, old folk leaving an almshouse, 'displaced persons', prisoners on trial, third-class travelers and the like. His sketch for an effigy of the Republic—which was not accepted—showed a mother suckling her children. On occasion, his sympathy gave place to banter; as when he turned his pen against print-collectors and prosecutors in the law-courts. But here satire is not his aim; he aims solely at a schematized yet total expression of character, reduced to its simplest, most telling elements, and the vigorous, personal handling of form and color speaks for a master's hand. Here, too, we see the goodness of heart that Forain referred to: but it is not that of a rich man handing out some of his spare cash, but that of a compassionate man who knows what human suffering is and wants to do what he can to ease it.

Moreover, Daumier in expressing his compassion achieved lyrical effects of the highest order. Historical subjects haunted him, and he even planned to paint the whole story of the Revolution. With this in view, he sought to rise above the mere representation of individual 'types' and specific events, towards the general and the universal. It was in a symbolic expression of the myth that he found a medium for the moral elevation to which he constantly aspired. And in the story of Don Quixote, the gentle-hearted, moonstruck idealist with whom he himself had so much in common, he found just what he needed. He planned to illustrate the whole book—in other words, retell the story—adding to it perhaps some of the epic grandeur lacking in this somewhat over-picaresque romance, but in keeping with his own nature and with his style.

The leading features of that wholly original style as exemplified in his painting are simplicity and nobility. Grave, subdued, excluding all trivial or garish tonalities, his color-schemes are in some ways similar to those of Corot, who had the same modesty and elegance of taste. The charm of Daumier's palette lies in his warm tones shot with glints of gold, the discreet chiaroscuro, and especially the light which, serenely flooding from above, engenders contrasts never harsh or jarring, but rich in mysterious intimations and poetic feeling.

MILLET AND THE SOIL

Millet was a Norman peasant from the Cotentin peninsula who had himself tilled the soil, and was never to forget it. Hence the vast sympathy he always felt for those who earn their living with the sweat of their brow. As a boy, in the evenings, after a hard day on the land, he would read with equal enthusiasm the Bible, Homer, Shakespeare, Byron, Goethe and Victor Hugo, not to mention Fenimore Cooper and Paul de Kock. He began sketching as a youth and, coming to Paris on a small grant, made his way at first by painting 'gallant' pictures in the manner of Boucher, not without success. But he also haunted the Louvre; he took his art seriously and soon gave up doing nudes, his renderings of which had met with considerable favor. Not forgetting the hard years of his early life, he also painted beggars, quarrymen, laborers and his admirable *Winnower*, which Ledru-Rollin purchased from him for five hundred francs. Finally he settled down at Barbizon and spent the remainder of his life there. His feeling for nature was deep and sincere, and had nothing of the vaguely theatrical attitudinizing we find in Rousseau. Always tinged with melancholy, his landscapes served as a setting for the actions of his figures: haymakers, sowers, washerwomen, reapers. Actually—and this was the true romantic streak in him—it was always himself he painted in the guise of his peasants.

At once a peasant and a seaman, for ever yearning for his humble village in Normandy, Millet had drifted to the famous forest with no set purpose and never felt really at home there. He did not paint the woodland for its own sake, as did Rousseau, but took of it just as much as served his turn: the few trees in his *Peasants Gathering Firewood*, for example. His real interest lay in harvesters, shepherds, reapers and their like, none of whom were to be seen in the forest.

There have been attempts to represent Millet as an ardent socialist, but he was nothing of the kind. Two revolutions took place in France in the course of his life. When a nation is divided against itself the partisans of one side or the other are only too eager to include amongst their supporters all those who they think may serve their cause, if not actively, by way of propaganda. Thus because Millet specialized in painting peasants, workers, the humble and unprivileged, many assumed that he had socialistic or even revolutionary leanings. No doubt the struggles of his youth and a life that had little happiness in it led him to tinge his pictures with his personal emotions, the melancholy which had become a second nature with him; but he always stood aloof from political agitation and those whom he called 'the people' had only a vague connection with the masses who are the makers of revolutions. He was neither a politician nor a moralist, and the humble folk of whom he was so fond, tillers of the soil eternal as the earth herself, were not those whose lot changes greatly with a change of social order. All he thought of was his painting, and he kept all his life long an attitude of independence not only towards men at large but towards art as well. Courbet, whose studio he frequented at one period, said: "He's a man of the backwoods sure enough, but he turns

It was only fairly late in life, when he was about thirty-four, that Millet, shaking off the influences of Correggio and Diaz, tackled rural subjects; this was just before he settled at Barbizon (in 1849). The sculptural form of *The Sower* has very rightly been compared to those figures illustrating scenes of rustic toil which we find on Gothic cathedrals. Here Millet painted man, alone in the vastness of the countryside, preparing for the harvest of the future. These same fields and these same immemorial gestures inspired Pissarro and Van Gogh to compositions no less moving than this famous picture. Van Gogh saw in Millet the true master of reality.

out good work, he invents muscles!" And, after inspecting one of his sketches, a quite early one, Delaroche said to him: "One can see you have done a lot of painting." Millet retained his independence vis-à-vis the great masters, too, and never copied them; though always loud in praises of Poussin, he reserved his right to criticize the work of that great landscapist. Unceasingly he sought to perfect a technique all his own. His drawing is at once vigorous and humbly faithful to life.

As we might expect, he kept to subdued, discreetly sober colors. Like Corot, and for the same reasons—modesty and discretion—he avoided any over-brilliant tones. Asking his friend Sensier to buy him colors, he wrote: "Send me three burnt Siennas, two ditto raw; three Naples yellows, two yellow ochres, two burnt umbers." He was blamed for using so dark a palette, and the Goncourts in their *Journal* speak of his "depressingly glaireous color." The truth is that Millet used the colors that honest observation showed him, and these necessarily lacked the romantic glamor and more immediate appeal of an 'art for art's sake.'

COURBET: BUILDER OF FORM

Conforming to the usual classification, we have included Daumier amongst the realists; we shall do the same for Courbet. Yet, in actual fact, the aesthetic standpoints, the temperaments and the procedures of the two great artists were utterly unlike.

GUSTAVE COURBET (1819-1877). WOMEN SIFTING CORN. (22 × 15″) MUSEUM, NANTES.

Courbet's peasants are racy of the soil, they have the stolid patience, the slow, deliberate strength that work on the land demands, season after season. We see a precise interpretation of this strength in the movement of the woman with the sieve. Her waist, whose slenderness is stressed so as to emphasize the massive shoulders, combines with the arms, the sieve and the slope of the back of her neck to form a perfect oval. Round this central volume the outspread skirt and the seated woman build up complementary volumes telling out against the verticals defining the secondary planes.

1930

JEAN-FRANÇOIS MILLET (1815-1875). THE WASH TUB, C. 1861. (17¼ × 13″) LOUVRE, PARIS.

FROM LE NAIN
TO CÉZANNE

Our aim *has been to give five telling examples of the wonderful variety of French 'realism' from its earliest instinctive forms to its most abstract developments. The conception of fidelity to the model involves the use of simple gestures and of forthright attitudes illustrating the essential rhythms of the body. Gesture is not used to externalize an emotion or for any ornamental end. That is why it calls for closely knit design, both to give it plastic value and to implement the lay-out of the picture in terms of volumes.*

LOUIS LE NAIN (1593-1648). PEASANT FAMILY IN AN INTERIOR, C. 1643. DETAIL. LOUVRE, PARIS.

Louis le nain, *Chardin and Millet probably had no wish to depict the 'picturesque' side of the peasant life of their day. They have recourse to models whose inner life is identical with their own. This explains the respect they show towards the model, and their avoidance of any ideal predetermined lay-out; rather we have here a sort of discretion, to which the composition owes its compelling power and grandeur. But this self-imposed simplicity led the artist, sensitive as he was, to give close attention to the lighting of his picture and to enliven its apparent monochrome by a skillful distribution of the 'values.'*

J. B. S. CHARDIN (1699-1779). THE DRAFTSMAN, 1738.
(7 ½ × 6¾″) NATIONAL MUSEUM, STOCKHOLM.

73a

THE AWARENESS OF REALITY

FRENCH ART *has always been profoundly influenced by the rich and fertile soil of France on which it thrived, and its very real devotion to nature is manifested in its constant awareness of reality. This is due to the deep love for nature inherent in the French temperament. It is not a patronizing or possessive love like that of the Italian masters. On the contrary, authentically French art always treats 'Dame Nature' on an equal footing; when necessary, the painter may show deference to her, as he has been advised to do, but he looks her squarely in the face, is on easy terms with her, while always ready to humor her foibles—and she returns his love. He goes even further, and identifies himself with the reality of ordinary men and common things. For, in the last analysis, this Realism derives from a tacit understanding between the individual, his everyday life and the world around him. Always there slumbers a peasant in the French heart, even the most sophisticated, and none is more realistic than the peasant, who chiefly asks of life that he should be free from fears and idle hopes alike, from emotional or intellectual predicaments. Provided his life runs smoothly, what matter if it be what the supercilious would call 'earthbound'? And our typical Frenchman instinctively mistrusts the imagination, as being a disturbing factor.*

This may explain why from its earliest days French art has always evoked, with a realism touched with a simple emotion, those purely human feelings we find in the mediaeval frescos, in Romanesque and Gothic statuary, in the faces of the Saints, of the Virgin and of Christ.

A CONSTANT IN FRENCH ART

CARVINGS, *capitals of pillars, stained-glass windows illustrate the life of tillers of the soil, craftsmen, farmyard animals, trees and flowers. Likewise those admirable 13th-century Books of Hours and the tapestries of the 14th and 15th centuries show us nature faithfully and sensitively rendered. Under the influence of a middle class which had no desire for heroic visions or imaginary scenes, the artist tended to represent real human beings whose physical appearance revealed their inner life, and to place them in simple settings, in which objects of everyday use are depicted with loving care. In the figures painted by Froment, Charonton and Fouquet, and, later, by the Clouets and Corneille de Lyon, we feel the artist's respect for, and comprehension of, his fellow men; he is faithful not only to his outward appearance but also to the personality of the man within with which it is bound up inseparably.*

Thus the French Realist never lapses into mere 'Naturalism.' He does not content himself with painting what he sees with his eyes but gets down to the soul of his model, and the reality he shows us is that which he perceives with his mind's eye. Refusing to accept any impediment to the free expression of his sensibility, he usually dispenses with those intellectual prescriptions—canons of beauty, strict proportions and mathematical procedures—on which Italian art set so much store, and, as a rule, trusts to the guidance of his instinct. Still, this does not prevent him from bearing in mind the organization and considered lay-out of the picture, called for by the nature of the subject.

CÉZANNE *stood for a new conception of reality, truer than that of appearances, "solid and abiding" as against the fugitive sensations of Impressionism, and stripped of all anecdotal elements. Once his intuitive analysis of the object had given him what he called his "little sensation," he went on to synthesize the various elements he had selected and fixed in his mind in view of their appropriateness to the general lay-out of the composition. But he never lost contact with the model, for he mistrusted the vagaries of the imagination. He remakes the object wholly with its own elements, but by re-arranging them he creates forms which have a value in themselves and adjust the data of reality to their ever more abstract patterns.*

PAUL CÉZANNE (1839-1906). THE CARD PLAYERS, 1892. (17 ¼ × 22″) LOUVRE, PARIS.

—

1932

1931

—

GUSTAVE COURBET (1819-1877). L'APRÈS-DINÉE A ORNANS, 1849. DETAIL. MUSEUM, LILLE.

GUSTAVE COURBET *was a painter who always saw reality in his own image and all his idiosyncrasies are apparent in his rendering of it. In this work the figures on the left are still romantically handled, whereas the man who is smoking, seated on the right, the volume of the hat, the planes and the perspective of the arms foreshadow Cézanne's architectural procedure. Courbet's concern was to render the appearance of things, the glow of their surface life. True, he adjusted them to his own vision and taste, but never 'prettified' or 'denatured' their essential form. And if he tends to simplify and stylize, this is due to his identification with the model. Courbet quite rightly termed his large compositions 'real-life allegories,' his* Studio *being a good example.*

73c

We often find that the work of an artist of an earlier generation takes a new lease of life and comes into fashion when it seems to be in line with contemporary anxieties and aspirations. Thus the period of violence, unrest and passionate ideologies in which we now are living has brought conspicuously into the limelight such artists as Caravaggio, Goya and Gustave Courbet, who underwent much the same emotional ordeals as those of the modern world today. It is not so much a matter of a revival of interest due to a passing fashion, as something inevitable and striking deeper; whether we like it or not, our artistic criteria are bound to be determined to some extent by the conditions of the world around us.

This may well explain why that remarkable man Courbet, who in his day was so cordially detested for his brutal intransigence both as a man and as an artist (though even then, it must be granted, he had some admirers), strikes us today as an almost likable personality, both for the glorious wealth of color he lavished on his pictures, and for the Rabelaisian 'gigantism' of the man himself, the naïve, extravagant audacity of his pretensions.

Physically, Courbet was one of those giants sometimes to be seen in the French countryside. He was handsome "as an Assyrian god", very tall, and had finely molded features, slotted, fascinating, almost feline eyes (as we see in a photograph by Nadar), a Semitic nose, a vast shock of hair, and a black, curly beard such as had not been seen on an artist since the days of Caravaggio. He had also an iron constitution. A great talker, great runner after women, great blusterer, he was great in everything—even in his stupidity, which he carried to such epic heights as to force our reluctant admiration. He was unself-conscious to the point of shamelessness, always brimming over with energy, and vastly pleased with himself; sometimes he had the intuitions of a man of genius, sometimes made remarks suggestive of a half-wit. All he had learnt from the desultory law studies of his early youth was the knack of being a law unto himself. And here we have one of the secrets of a 'realism' quite different from Daumier's, stemming solely from his libertarian temperament.

Courbet was born in 1819, at Ornans, in the Franche-Comté, the province of old France whose capital is Besançon. His father, a prosperous vinegrower, was something of a dreamer on Utopian lines. His grandfather, an ancient follower of Voltaire, brought the child up according to his own ideas; that is to say, he was left free to roam the countryside as he thought fit. Sent to the small seminary of Ornans, he was the despair of his masters; he showed a complete lack of interest in his lessons (all his life he loathed books) and already began to profess anti-religious sentiments which (if he is to be believed) caused quite a flutter in the dovecotes of the local Bishop's Palace. While still a boy he tried his hand at drawing and painting and took some lessons from a Besançon painter named Flageoulot. But he learnt little from his teacher; he was one of those who seem to know everything without being taught. In fact Courbet was what is called a 'force of Nature,' a fertile soil in which tares and good grain thrived side by side, as the wind chanced to strew the seeds. And, again naturally enough, his taste for bigness of all kinds led him to depicting giant trees, huge rocks, and monumental bodies.

GUSTAVE COURBET (1819-1877). THE ARTIST'S STUDIO, C. 1855. DETAIL. LOUVRE, PARIS.

Courbet called this a 'real-life allegory.' But in order to appreciate this huge canvas, each part of which is an admirable *morceau* of painting, we have no need to inquire into the esoteric meanings he intended it to convey. In his handling of the woman in the Indian shawl (whom we find again in Renoir), the artist showed a strong, vigorous hand, while his touch is all delicacy and nuance when he treats the pair of lovers sinking into shadow, and the woman wearing a 'Pekin' dress (a figure we later find in Manet). To the right of the couple in the foreground is Baudelaire, to the left Champfleury, the first champion of Courbet's art. In the center of the picture we have the triumphant figure of Courbet himself, looking like a king surrounded by his courtiers and, so to speak, escorted by several of his own admirable 'bravura pieces.' Despite the great boldness of the composition, the perfect unity of this work compels our admiration.

That he always liked the company of peasants, workers and humble folk can be explained by his innate attachment to the land and simple, almost rustic manners. It certainly was not due, as in kindly Daumier's case, to any real feeling of compassion. Not that he was hard-hearted. But, for one thing, his family was well-off and moreover, at bottom, he was an anarchist. Thus his interest in the 'lower classes' was of an intellectual order. It was not a sense of pity that led him to paint his famous *Stonebreakers*; it was simply a desire to fly in the face of authority and to air his views. For he had an egotism, an immense vanity, of which he made no secret. He once said to his friend Silvestre, the eminent critic: "How I'd have enjoyed rescuing the woman I loved from a house on fire, with ten thousand people goggling their eyes at me; I'd not have felt half so good about it if nobody were looking on." Thus his seeming humanitarianism had little in common with Daumier's, had not his approach to reality. Daumier served reality, Courbet put it to his service. So much so that he protested against being labeled a 'realist,' saying he was a 'Courbetist' and nothing else. His political activities were those of a hothead; what were his real convictions, if any, remains a mystery. He was accused of having helped to tear down the Vendôme Column (during the Commune), and probably he did; it would have been quite in keeping with his taste for violent physical activity.

But all this 'sound and fury' was extrinsic to the real Courbet, the man within, the artist whose genius is manifest in all his work, a free expression of the instinctual drive of a painter pure and simple. In his art he was utterly sincere, a man in the thrall of a *grande passion*. In spite of his narcissistic disregard of everything outside himself, he often visited the art-museums; the temptation was too strong. True, when he entered these temples of high art, he took care to assume an air of philistine disdain. In the presence of Michelangelo he guffawed; he damned Titian and Raphael for arrant rogues, adding: "If either of that pair came back to life and showed up in my studio, I'd get my knife out!" The only masters he would have spared were Veronese, Velazquez and, oddly enough, Holbein. Amongst his contemporaries, David was merely "a reactionary who hamstrung painting," and the art of Delacroix was "a mere pandemonium of forms." And he had even harder words for Ingres and Corot.

In short, Courbet the artist was far superior to Courbet the man. To begin with, he is instinct pure and simple. And he loved nature in his way—with a possessive love. It is amazing to see with what zest, what happy inspiration, this pure materialist, a romantic despite himself, remakes nature; and how that 'intelligence' of which he was always boasting played no part at all in the creative act. He could work only at high pressure, driven on by an inner demon of unrest. On those occasions when he lost grip, out of sheer fatigue, and the tension flagged, the effect was promptly visible in his work; it grew petrified, inert. But such occasions were rare. The driving force behind it redeems the chaos of his composition. The texture of his brushwork has an amazing richness and diversity; sometimes, we must admit, a certain vulgarity. His form and color are usually on the heroic scale; they give a truth to plastic reality, an intensity, a depth that are wholly admirable. Yet, boor though he was in so many ways, Courbet could show amazing delicacy on occasion; in those gentler moods when the child within him came to the fore, he painted in nuances of the most exquisite tenderness and charm. The truth is he worked without any plan; he never stopped to think, and tolerated no rules, no constraints. He let his instinct try its luck, and, be it said, brought off the *coup*. This is perhaps why so many painters, whatever their tendencies, join in admiring Courbet, and doubtless envy him in their heart of hearts.

GUSTAVE COURBET (1819-1877). LA TOILETTE DE LA MARIÉE, 1860. SMITH COLLEGE MUSEUM OF ART, NORTHAMPTON, MASSACHUSETTS.

In this large canvas, which he left in an unfinished state, Courbet has recorded the wedding preparations in a well-to-do peasant family of the Franche-Comté. He has omitted nothing, not even the traditional bowl of cheese soup a woman is placing on the table. Since he did not carry it through to the end, this picture gives us a good idea of Courbet's methods: he began by laying in thick dabs of pigment with the palette-knife, and added the details later.

4

AN AMBIANCE OF FORMS AND SENSATIONS

COROT - ROUSSEAU - COURBET

MANET - DEGAS - WHISTLER

JONGKIND - BOUDIN

MONET - RENOIR - PISSARRO - SISLEY

THE AUTONOMY *of the landscape as a* genre *existing in its own right was now assured, and artists applied themselves assiduously to investigating its problems, each in his own way. Nature was no longer treated as a mere setting. The 'landscape-state of mind' was now the touchstone of the artist's personality, and he interpreted it according to his temperament and his vision of the world. Corot was so devotedly in love with nature that all his life long he applied himself to registering the impressions nature made on him and rendering them in their pristine purity. The painters of the School of Barbizon and Courbet acquired a profound knowledge of the life of the earth and the forests, but the problem of rendering the translucence of the atmosphere was not solved until a little later, with the coming of Impressionism, which, while taking over the empirical discoveries of Jongkind and Boudin, implemented these by scientific investigations into the breaking-up of light, the 'rainbow palette.' Thus the variations in nature's aspects due to the passing hours could be recorded with a precision hitherto undreamt-of. It was assumed that by an ever more intensive analysis of visual experience a still more accurate vision could be attained. This was an illusion; for the effect of such procedure is merely to water down the true impression. The most lasting contribution made by Impressionism was a prodigious improvement on the technical side of painting. And with the close of the century and Cézanne's declaration of his wish "to make Impressionism something solid and abiding like the old masters," there were signs of a desire to restore to painting its rendering of the structure of nature and its underlying geometric pattern, in terms of volumes and planes of color.*

THE FRENCH LANDSCAPE

Since the days of the Gothic illuminated manuscripts and the Primitives, French landscape-painting had almost lost the realist feeling for nature, which was to come back only gradually. It began by following new conceptions that differed with the time, the place and the artists. As treated by such Italian masters as Giorgione, Titian and, above all, Giovanni Bellini, landscape was monumental, and always divided into fragments; though, no doubt, a certain atmosphere gave it life, it was, essentially, an arrangement of masses in space in terms of purely plastic rhythms. El Greco's landscapes are dramatic visions inspired by the artist's mystical emotion; while Rubens builds his up into strange, architectural patterns, to express a world of his own imagining. In the work of the 17th-century Dutch masters, with whom we first feel landscape coming into its own as an independent form of art, a certain realism crept in and, by the use of chiaroscuro, light began to play a more explicit role. Patinir, that simple and moving artist, sought to render atmosphere above all else.

Always engrossed in problems of composition, Poussin, too, gave thought to pure landscape, even in his *Historical Landscape* and notably in *Polyphemus* and *Diogenes with a Bowl*, admirable works that figure forth enchanted wonderlands. But these were still creations of the mind. With Claude Lorrain we come to landscape pure and simple; for all the figures in his luminous compositions were probably the work of another hand.

Thus it was that landscape-painting moved steadily towards the landscape painted for its own sake. Even so, it remained descriptive, a kind of architectural décor, more and more cluttered up with detail. And at the end of the 18th century academicism made matters worse by indulging in Valenciennes' *beau feuillé* and foisting the anecdotal on the landscape. Only when painters' eyes really opened to nature did landscape get a new lease of life. But there came first a period inspired by Rousseau and Chateaubriand: landscapists painted charming but quite unconvincing scenes in which nature was tinkered with, improved on, glossed over and peopled with beribboned shepherd girls and peasants in their Sunday best, with happy farms and dairies in the best Trianon style. Painters like Hubert Robert (1733-1808), d'Aligny (1798-1878), Valenciennes (1750-1819), Demarne (1754-1829) and de Boissieu (1736-1810) are languorous, artificial, decorative. Their landscapes were perfectly suited to painting on porcelain-ware and as such became immensely popular. With them all sentiment was sentimentality: the influence of the English landscapists had not yet made itself felt.

Georges Michel (1769-1843) is perhaps the only French painter of this period who had genuine feeling for nature as she really is, and accepted her as such. In him Constable's remark that "nothing in nature is ugly," seems to have found an echo. It is true that Michel's art still aims to some extent at an idealized imitation of nature. With him reality remains impersonal; it is not yet seen through the medium of a poetic temperament of a truly personal order.

THE BALANCE OF COROT

Only with Corot (1796-1875) was landscape given an expression capable of proving it to be no longer a theme of secondary interest for art, but worthy to rank beside the portrait and the human body. Furthermore, Corot, so long regarded exclusively as a landscapist, showed himself to be also a master of the human figure, for his genius was many-sided, he was interested in all the forms of life. In this connection, Gustave Geffroy made an illuminating observation: "Corot paints his figures like landscapes."

Unlike those of so many contemporary painters, Corot's life was simple and uneventful. He was born in Paris, rue du Bac; his father, an accountant, came from Burgundy and his mother was French-Swiss. He saw high school through to the age of nineteen without having shown any great interest in his studies. His parents were excellent folk who would have liked to see their boy enter business. But when he rebelled against this, they gave in, and consented to his becoming an artist, although that walk of life was then regarded with much disfavor. In appearance, Corot was tall, athletically built, bursting with health. His strong features told of good nature, simplicity and gaiety. All for a simple life, he never worried. He was perfectly contented, providing he was free to feast his eyes on nature whenever so inclined, could steer clear of sentimental entanglements (while indulging in occasional liaisons with French or Italian girls), enjoy a comfortable income, and, so far as art was concerned, keep to the path he had mapped out—a very simple one—without being troubled by soul-searchings or intellectual doubts. His friend Delecluze reported him as saying that "no one does really fine work by going to infinite pains." And he voiced his own wonderful serenity of mind in a famous remark: "I don't seek, I lie in wait."

But we should be wrong to visualize Corot as a plaster saint, possessing all the obvious virtues: goodness of heart, gentleness, modesty and so forth. It is quite enough that the appellation 'Père Corot,' endearing enough but making him seem slightly ridiculous, has been foisted on him. Some (Paul Valéry included) have likened him to Virgil, others to "that worthy man" La Fontaine—a dubious comparison when we remember what the "worthy man" showed himself to be in his works and in his private life. All this would have been quite in keeping had Corot been merely a landscapist in a small way, as a number of his friends were. But the man who said: "Roughness is better in a beginner than softness," was not so easy-going as all that. Moreover he was anything but a puritan, and liable to fits of anger on occasion. And there is that story of a 'secret cupboard,' allegedly containing reminiscences of a somewhat lurid order.

Corot began his career by entering into friendly relations with several academic-minded painters: Valenciennes, Bertin, d'Aligny, and particularly Bidault and Michallon, who gave him much useful advice. He made three visits to Italy where his eyes were opened to the great classical tradition, as well as to the 'tricks of the trade' used in the historical landscape. In the architecture, the ruins and the gardens of Rome he found inspiration for a method of balancing of masses in full light, such as we find in his

CAMILLE COROT (1796-1875). PORTRAIT OF THE ARTIST, 1835. (13 × 9¾") UFFIZI, FLORENCE.

Corot himself presented this picture to the Uffizi Gallery, which had asked him for a work. Gone here is the sense of strain we feel in the 1826 portrait. The arrangement of the face and bust on the canvas, the use of two oval volumes formed by the cap and the palette, the harmony between their somber tonality and the luminous effect of the work as a whole—all this pointed the way to a new science of composition.

Pont San Bartolommeo (1826), a picture destined to excite so much comment, and whose delicate precision of light-effects he only surpassed some twenty years later in his *Bridge at Mantes*. Corot had a special fondness for the arches of bridges, an ideal setting for his subtle interpretations of the play of light and shadow. The possibilities of light fascinated him and, as his friends had been unable to teach him much about it, he discovered, or rediscovered for himself, the secrets of this side of painting. Thus, with great skill he played off tones against each other; certain details he blurred in light, the better to rivet attention on what he regarded as essential points. By eliciting its simplest elements, he sought to get down to the very essence of the object; avoiding glaring colors and over-simplified contrasts, he allocated 'values' with a care indicative of the high importance he attached to them.

Thus he steadily built up his technique, while his outlook on nature grew ever more precise. Corot understood nature well, and drew his inspiration from his innate love for her. In her presence, he did not use his imagination, but gave himself up to contemplation, then closed his eyes, one would say, so as to re-create within what he saw without. He approached her with some misgivings to begin with, then growing bolder, was soon on intimate terms with her. Indeed, Corot identified himself with nature; it never crossed his mind merely to imitate her; as indeed is evident from the 'harmonist' tonalities he came to use, and for which he was much blamed.

"Just being one's self is the only way to move others," he once said; he wished to impart his feelings, not to arouse admiration. In the days of Monteverdi, before the metronome had been invented, time in music was measured by the pulse-beat, and this was referred to as *tempo naturale*. This way of measuring rhythm brings Corot to mind and illustrates, in a manner of speaking, his self-made 'golden section.' For in his painting he seems to go ahead, with no preconceived ideas. More a builder than an architect, he had much in him of the rural stonemason who builds his house with an innate sense of just proportion that astounds the professional architect. Like Constable he might have said that in nature's presence his first concern was to forget ever having seen a painting. Corot, no doubt, went one better, and never thought about it at all. Moreover he never tried to mask his lapses; he "fixed them up with a deft touch at the danger spot," as he quite ingenuously told a friend. It is an interesting fact that Corot

CAMILLE COROT (1796-1875). VIEW OF ROME; THE COLISEUM. 1825-1826. (9 × 13″) LOUVRE, PARIS.

Corot was always fond of the arches of bridges and vaulted arcades, whose structure is an ideal medium for the dissemination of light and shade. We have here a good example of this: a geometrical, almost abstract composition in which the artist analyses the variations of light in terms of a sequence of its varying intensities, due to the superimposed planes and the spacing out in depth of plastic elements that condense or magnify the brightness of the scene.

was the first painter to use the word "impression." And he brought out the meaning when he said: "What we feel is as real as anything else." The sentiment expressed was something quite new in painting and we may wonder at its coming from an artist who showed so much respect for the classical rules, anyhow in his early days. Never, even in the most pantheistic effusion of its love of nature, had Romanticism attained such depth of feeling as Corot did. And how simple and sincere, how human, was his conception of art! He had the same aversion for 'loud' colors as he had for raising the tone of his voice in conversation. He always drew a veil of grey over the harsher passages; his is an art of greys with undertones of pink, green, ochre and blue. He does not so

CAMILLE COROT (1796-1875). THE BRIDGE AT MANTES, 1868-1870. (14½ × 22″) LOUVRE, PARIS.

Moving away from the clear-cut outlines of his Italian landscapes, Corot developed that 'hazy' manner which was to be his personal contribution to the conquest of light. He boldly challenged tradition by intersecting the foreground with bare tree-trunks whose vertical lines set up a kind of syncopated rhythm dominating the whole composition. To the background is thus imparted an unlooked-for vitality, a sudden animation, mysteriously augmented by the twigs and branches whose function it is to striate the light and distribute its intensity.

1936

For a long time the human element in Corot's art was belittled and even ridiculed. We can see now, however, that his figures are nowise inferior to his finest landscapes. The correctness of their values and the simplicity of their volumes enable them to stand comparison with those of Vermeer. Corot painted them for his own pleasure from living models; he never felt called upon to invent a subject or to locate them in a recognizable scene of daily life.

much render color as establish harmony. And grey, we might say, is the local color of his natural modesty. Always, too, he simplifies, with a vigorous hand and an innate skill.

The affection all other painters have for Corot is a proof of his immense influence. Many famous masters are beloved, but Corot above all. Though he wrote little and spoke less, some of his observations pointed towards new paths in art, undreamt-of even by himself. "Let us never lose that first fine impression which has moved us," was one of them. Here we have a first step towards Impressionism. The perfection of his painted sketches shows that the 'snapshot' of his first impression was enough, and explains why he could look back on these works in later days without finding the least element foreign to his original emotion. Thus, his was not an Impressionism of the kind that gives the mere photographic likeness of an object, but the expression of an inward vision transcending external reality so as to create another, for him more real. Corot was no copyist of nature; he made his own 'nature.'

THE SCHOOL OF BARBIZON

In the second half of the 18th century, the Forest of Fontainebleau was already known to artists. For this we have the word of Louis XVI, who one day remarked: "As we crossed the forest I saw no one but Bruandet, and some wild boars"—Bruandet being a contemporary painter who failed to make his name despite this bit of royal publicity. It was in 1830 that Corot came to Fontainebleau for the first time, but for him one landscape was as good as another; indeed, to this romantic forest, with its huge rock-formations, immemorial trees and luxuriant vegetation, he preferred a few silver-birches standing apart, filtering the sunlight through their shimmering foliage. None the less, the forest village of Barbizon became the happy hunting-ground of artists on the look out for 'impressions.' There, between 1830 and 1875, we find Diaz, Chintreuil, Daubigny, Dupré, Troyon and others, but above all Millet and Rousseau, who spent the best part of their lives around Fontainebleau and died there. The artists used to forgather at the famous *Auberge du Père Ganne*, which they only quit to go off to work in the depths of the forest, that wild, unkempt forest in whose likeness they grew their famous bison-beards *(barbes de bison)*, which in a popular song of the day was rhymed to 'Barbizon.'

In some of its aspects the School of Barbizon remained under the influence of Romanticism. Nevertheless the landscape treated as a reflection of a mood tended to disappear; these painters were not visionaries but men who genuinely loved Nature and delighted in observing her. No doubt they always tended to embellish what they saw, but they never idealized it, still less stylized it, as their predecessors, the practitioners of the 'historical landscape' had done. In rendering a scene of nature they intensified its life, its power and majesty or its gentle charm, but they never went to the point of distorting it, 'denaturing' it. Though in the poetic art of Rousseau and Millet all is strictly in keeping with their respective temperaments (imbued with power and majesty in the case of Rousseau, with quiet emotion in the art of Millet), both alike aim at an objective representation of the outside world, and endeavor to express the rich, earthy tang of the soil, the strange enchantments of the forest, the expressive value of the light, the laborious lives of the peasantry. They do this quite straightforwardly, without recourse to the more or less artificial procedures of the Romantics, who so often and so brilliantly camouflage reality. The Barbizon masters take Nature seriously; they do not regard her as a pretext for painting, still less as a source-book, Delacroix's famous 'dictionary.' For them she is the incarnation of an all-pervading presence, which they are half inclined to deify after the manner of the myth-makers of antiquity. We are reminded of certain ritual processions, that of the 'Rogations' for example, in which divine favor is invoked for an abundant harvest. Thus the Barbizon painters concur in glorifying Nature as the Lady Bountiful, dispenser of all man needs here below, and their faith in her was total and unfaltering.

Hence that religious sentiment which we feel to underlie the art of the French landscapists. Indeed each of their works is an act of homage to Mother Earth, whose

With Rousseau painting quitted the studio and came out into the open air; Corot, however, continued to think the studio necessary for the 'finish' of the work. This picture shows old Montmartre and its windmills, only one of which, the Moulin de la Galette, remains today. Here the artist is less concerned with giving each element of the landscape its significance than in creating an atmosphere of violence in which every detail, briefly indicated by a deft brushstroke, is submerged.

sons are all mankind. And it is true to say that these artists, in so doing, express one of the most essential characteristics of the French sensibility.

Theodore Rousseau was a strapping, full-blooded young man, impressionable and warm-hearted, but domineering, "with the air of a black bull of the Jura country," as his friend, T. Silvestre, described him. He was always bubbling over with new ideas on art, all of which he regarded as inspired, though actually they were nebulous to a degree. He could not bear being contradicted and Millet meekly bowed his head and listened when he expounded his theories, explaining how "parallels draw together on the horizon when you're standing with the sun behind you," and so forth. But at heart he was a good fellow, simple and kind. His bombastic way of holding forth was the result of genuine enthusiasm and reflected his preference for the grandiose in nature, for solemn, majestic scenes. Far be it from him to set up his easel just anywhere, "even in front of a dunghill," as Courbet advised! On the contrary, he needed wide horizons, vast skies, towering trees, forest glades revealing depths on depths. The romantic side of Rousseau's temperament stems from this natural penchant for grandeur of every kind, and his technique is in accordance with his aspirations. He was fond of talking about his 'subjectivism.' In his view the composition of a picture should never follow any predetermined plan. The composition, he said, comes into being the moment the elements of visual experience cease to exist objectively and express the emotions they have inspired. It must be admitted that Rousseau's theories often seem rather muddled or anyhow expressed in an obscure way. Baudelaire said of Rousseau that he was "pestered by a thousand demons and never knew which to listen to." Sometimes Rousseau analyses the structure of nature aridly, neither trying to idealize nor to embellish it; on these occasions his 'subjectivism' seems to yield to a thoroughly objective realism, in which the part, if any, played by his emotions fails to make itself apparent. But as a rule he treats natural scenes in a broad, robust manner, full of imaginative inventiveness and bearing the stamp of his buoyant temperament. On the rare occasions when the human figure appears in his landscapes, it is no more than a trivial detail. This peculiarity of Rousseau is probably due to his typically romantic response to the sublime immensity of Nature, which roused in him both a sense of exaltation—indeed of personal superiority—and a corresponding feeling of the insignificance of mankind at large.

The influence of the Barbizon School on European art made itself felt rapidly and in various manners. Oddly enough it is in Holland that we find its first manifestation. Millet had shown his pity for the peasants, and Israels followed suit by depicting the sad condition of his co-religionists, while Anton Mauve and Mesdag, keeping in line with national 17th-century traditions, were profoundly affected by the art of Rousseau and Troyon.

In Germany Max Liebermann came under the spell of the Barbizon School, before being influenced by Impressionism. The Swedish painter Wahlberg depicted scenes of his country in the rather arid manner of Daubigny. The Hungarian Ladislas de Paal also settled at Barbizon in 1874, and owed much to Rousseau.

The Barbizon School influenced several Belgian painters: Fournois, Lamorinière, and Edmond de Schampheleer, and notably Alfred de Knyff (1829-1885), who drew inspiration from Rousseau, Dupré and Daubigny.

But it was in the United States that the School of Barbizon had the most noteworthy effects. William Morris Hunt (who studied under Millet), Troyon (a pupil of Daubigny) as well as George Inness, Homer and H. Martin, all put in a stay in France and met the leading figures of the School, whose directives they followed in a general way, while adjusting them to the different conditions of the American scene.

TRIUMPH OF THE OPEN AIR

The years between 1856 and 1863 were important ones, for it was then that a significant change occurred which was to open new horizons to the artist. The Romanticists, the English painters and the Barbizon School had all proposed a new approach to nature. Taken by the new notion of landscape which Amiel described as a "state of mind," artists began to set up their easels on the spot, under the open sky, in front of the 'motif.' Still, they did this half-heartedly; they were not yet at ease in dealing with changing aspects of nature, due to the variations in the light. Yet Constable had shown how this could be done, and after him the Barbizon painters, who drew from nature and sometimes sketched out the canvas in the open air, though they always retreated to the studio to supply the finishing touches.

Artists grew gradually bolder, however. More and more they took to using bright colors and were thus led to look the sunlight in the face and to discern in it a very real and living manifestation whose every form and aspect was worth the painter's study. And study it they did. Thus Courbet, with his *Girls on the Banks of the Seine*, and Manet, with his *Déjeuner sur l'herbe*, combined the two methods, painting the landscape itself directly from nature out of doors, but adding the figures in the seclusion of the studio. (Monet, however, was an exception; he painted his *Women in the Garden* entirely in the open air.) But this way of working was unsatisfactory: the practice of incorporating the figures in the landscape did not give convincing results, and the composition lacked unity. It is true that Boudin 'stuck' figures on to his seascapes, but with him these were in the nature of mere annotations that merged perfectly into the scene. With Manet, Monet and Renoir this was impossible, owing to the size of their figures, which, it must be admitted, are rather like large silhouettes plastered on to a stiff and lifeless landscape. There is no free play of atmosphere, and the light is merely 'lighting.' And as the vogue for bright colors steadily increased, they did not hesitate to indulge in color patterns motley to the point of garishness. Yet even so, in works of this period, we feel that some of the classical procedures are respected. Rules of perspective, for instance, and those of local color, were still adhered to. These artists still made use of chiaroscuro and the light, not yet diffused throughout the picture, seems to issue from a single source. In short these works lacked the audacity that came in a few years later, when the Impressionists, having learnt the secrets of the light and air that had stifled and dazzled them at first, could look back on the pictures combining open-air with studio work, and perceive the shortcomings of that procedure, its essential lack of truth to nature.

Still, the fact remains that the practice of open-air painting was never accepted whole-heartedly by all artists. Thus Renoir once said to Vollard: "I was fortunate enough to be with Corot one day; I mentioned to him my difficulty in working out of doors. His answer was as follows: 'The fact is that, in the open air, you can never be sure of what you're doing. It's best to finish off in the studio'." This from Corot, who rendered nature with a truth and lifelikeness no Impressionist ever achieved!

1939

GUSTAVE COURBET (1819-1877). GIRLS ON THE BANKS OF THE SEINE, 1856. (68 × 81″)
LOUVRE, PARIS.

THIS CORUSCATING PICTURE *was one of those which did most to persuade the Impressionists-to-be of the advantages of painting in the open air. It was, moreover, Courbet's fondness for bright colors, so apparent here, that encouraged the younger artists to investigate the possibilities of rendering that authentic light of day which was capable both of imparting greater unity to the picture, and at the same time giving a more faithful and realistic interpretation of nature. In his* Déjeuner sur l'herbe, *however, Manet, whose work was entering on the transitional phase, from Realism to Impressionism, still kept to Courbet's procedures in some respects.*

THIS FAMOUS PAINTING *was rejected by the official Salon of 1863 and then exhibited at the 'Salon des Refusés.' A charge of indecency was leveled against Manet, but his opponents were put to confusion when they learned that he had taken the theme from a 16th-century print,* The Judgement of Paris, *engraved after Raphael. The artist's avowed aim, however, was to give a modern version of Giorgione's* Fête champêtre. *Here he tackled a new problem. When first sketching out the work, he said: "It seems that I am expected to do a nude. Well, I'll give them one made in the* transparency of the atmosphere." *This was a new expression in the vocabulary of painting. And in fact Manet did paint the background of the picture directly from nature. The figures, however, as is quite obvious, were painted in the studio. For the lighting of the group in the foreground he used the same procedures as Courbet in his* Girls on the Banks of the Seine.

EDOUARD MANET (1832-1883). LE DÉJEUNER SUR L'HERBE, 1863. (82¾ × 106″) LOUVRE, PARIS.

1942

In THIS PICTURE, *for the first time, Manet chose a subject from contemporary life and in the elegant crowd we recognize several of the artist's friends, writers and painters, Fantin-Latour, Théophile Gautier and Baudelaire. At the time, critics and public alike were shocked by his quite unprecedented rendering of the subject, elliptically, in distinct patches of color. This work is a good example of that use of bright colors which the Impressionists were soon to turn to such good account. Later on, in his* Moulin de la Galette, *Renoir gave new intensity to this technique of using patches of color and thus pointed the way to the coming experiments in the division of tones.*

Holiday outings in the parks and gardens in and around Paris were a favorite theme, for they enabled the artists to come to grips with the problems of open-air painting. Manet's Concert at the Tuileries Gardens *(c. 1860) and Monet's* Women in the Garden *(1867) are characteristic examples of the artists' tendencies. Manet, for his part, has yielded here to his painterly instinct. His composition is an aggregate of strongly contrasted patches, but their arrangement was governed by no predetermined plan. The work is like an impression hastily jotted down, and a shade conventional; for it is redolent of the studio. It has not the structurally ordered composition which Manet, when faithful to tradition and to museum-art, so often gives us. This picture had a cool reception. The artist's friends took exception to the subject itself, regarded as rather too bold a choice, and also to the brightness of the colors. Even the quality of the painting was called into question and Baudelaire himself had qualms about it. To many the admirable* morceaux *in the foreground seemed uncalled for, and in fact the work in general was too much of an innovation to be whole-heartedly accepted even by Manet's friends and supporters.*

Monet aspired to steal a march on Manet, and the whole of his Women in the Garden *was painted out of doors, though not with entire success, we must admit. Here Monet seems to have worked out of doors just as he would have in his studio, with a model before him.*

The influence of Courbet is still dominant in this work, the Courbet of the rich and iridescent color we find in his Girls on the Banks of the Seine. *We may say, too, that while in his* Concert at the Tuileries Gardens, *Manet did not yet succeed in achieving (assuming he had this in mind at this stage of his career) that 'atmospheric transparency' of which he spoke, Monet cannot be said to have succeeded any better, assuming he was aiming at it here. For all its elaborate play of glints of light and the absence of strong contrasts, the distribution of light in the picture is due solely to the predetermined 'lighting.' Still Monet has the problem well in hand. His eyes have been opened to sunlight, though he still handles it in a conventional fashion, directing it this way and that like the beam of a searchlight. A year or two had yet to pass before the problem found its solution; when Monet and Renoir painted their famous* Grenouillères, *in which for the first time impressionist methods were successfully applied.*

CLAUDE MONET (1840-1926). WOMEN IN THE GARDEN, 1867. DETAIL. LOUVRE, PARIS.

THE THEME *of the race-meeting with its crowd of spectators, its jockeys and horses had already been used by Géricault, Carle Vernet, Alfred de Dreux and Eugène Lamy. And, indeed, these artists took special pleasure in watching horses in action. For them it was the most dynamic of subjects and its possibilities gripped their imagination. They remembered how Bouffon had spoken of that "noblest conquest of man," "the proud and fiery animal who shared with him the grimmest days of war and the glories of battle." Their passion for horses was kept alive by Delacroix. And now Manet and Degas exchanged their views on the problems raised by the racecourse theme, though neither (as our Plates make clear) was convinced by the other's arguments.*

Nevertheless, in a general way, their views coincided. Neither was in the least attracted either by the romantic tradition attaching to the horse, or by the sporting aspects of racing. Indeed, horses as such held no interest for them. They seem to have been drawn to the racetrack simply by the wonderful opportunity it offered: a brilliant, open-air spectacle containing in variety all the technical problems that had arisen, now that the virtues of studio-painting had been called into question. Both painters were, moreover, at one in their predilection for such scenes as these, the rendez-vous of fashionable society. This taste, due no doubt to their social background, was shared by Toulouse-Lautrec; whereas their impressionist friends took no interest in such subjects. One great difference between Manet and Degas is that the former has a penchant for analysis, the latter for synthesis.

Thus, in Manet's picture, there is no question of a realistic treatment of the scene. He has used his visual experience as a pretext for depicting a whirl of patches of color spangling a field of light. This seeming confusion admirably conveys the sensation of speed which the scene evoked in the artist; here he had an ideal opportunity for exploiting the vivacity and lightness of his expressive brushwork.

EDOUARD MANET (1832-1883). RACES AT LONGCHAMP, 1864. ART INSTITUTE, CHICAGO.

1944

EDGAR DEGAS (1834-1917). GENTLEMEN'S RACE, BEFORE THE START, 1862. (18 × 24")
LOUVRE, PARIS.

DEGAS *was always eager to try his hand at subjects involving special problems for the painter, and here he analyses the theme in all its details. His unrivaled gift for realistic accuracy has served him in good stead; the scene comes vividly to life under his brush, and he combines a quite amazing artistry with dynamism. But Degas never lost sight of the architectural arrangement of the composition; he always kept his technical ingenuity well in hand, however great the temptation to push his methods to extremes. Thus the smoking factory chimneys in the distance are not merely 'anecdotal'; they add an accent at a point where the lay-out called for it. And the figure groups which for technical reasons might have been treated as mere patches, are rendered in minute detail, with that superb craftsmanship Degas always had at his command.*

REALITY OF THE PICTURE

After the great pathfinders of the first half of the century came Manet, in whom we have yet another innovator. He has been called a virtuoso, which would make of him no more than a brilliant executant of others' works; but Manet was very much more than that. Before proceeding further, we do well to bear in mind that, in the second half of the century, a spirit of adventurousness resulting from the new cult of freedom was abroad among French artists, no matter what their social class. While Millet, for example, was of humble peasant extraction, Courbet was the son of a prosperous vine-grower. Manet came of an upper-class family with strict ideas of what was fitting. And rather than have him embark on the less perilous career of an artist, his worthy parents preferred to see him take ship for the Americas as a sixteen-year-old navigating cadet. Upon his return, however, finding their son as determined as ever to be an artist, the Manets gave in with a good grace, and consented to his studying art in Couture's atelier. But very soon he broke with his teacher as a result of the latter's unkind remark: "You'll never be more than the Daumier of your time." This was a blessing in disguise, for now, left free to choose, he turned instinctively to those true masters from whom he had so much to learn. From his twentieth year on, Manet traveled about Europe and came to know its museums thoroughly. For the time being, he studied Titian, Rembrandt, Tintoretto, and even Delacroix; it was only later on that he discovered Japanese art. He copied the works of the masters, but, even at this early stage, put much of himself into these copies. For he interpreted rather than imitated the originals; his program was to do them over again in a modern setting and on strictly painterly lines—as in his celebrated *Déjeuner sur l'herbe*, the theme of which he took from Titian and Giorgione and which the Emperor, Napoleon III, proclaimed "immodest."

It was this picture that roused critics and public, not to mention many painters, to attacks even more virulent than those that Ingres, Delacroix and Courbet in their day had to face. In the end, however, after the Salon had flatly rejected the *Déjeuner*, feelings ran so high that the Emperor was compelled to inaugurate the famous 'Salon des Refusés' (1863), where Manet exhibited alongside Jongkind, Fantin-Latour, Pissarro, Constable and Whistler. The charge of "immodesty" leveled at the *Déjeuner* was, of course, no more than a pretext; it was Manet's bold handling of color to which objection had really been taken. Especially singled out for attack was his lively and lifelike treatment of nature and his juxtapositions of bright colors without transitions, a practice condemned by Couture and the Academy, who believed in the traditional use of discreetly modulated bridgework between the tracts of brighter color. We shall see presently the consequence of this, one of Manet's boldest, most startling innovations. Next, in 1865, he exhibited his *Olympia* and a new wave of invective broke over his head. This time it was the alleged realism of the work that infuriated the critics. Idealism, that fetish of an earlier age, was long in dying, and the nude in *Olympia*, so free of any facile artifice, so frankly human in its starkness, could not fail to outrage those who still

THIS *is one of the works by Manet which most fully justify us in regarding him as an innovator of the first rank. This picture was rejected by the 1866 Salon, for fear of yet another scandal. In his famous article in the newspaper* L'Evénement *(May, 1866) Zola vigorously defended* The Fifer, *describing it as "a deliciously naïve, translucent work, charming to the point of seductiveness, real to the point of ruthlessness." Obviously in* The Fifer *Manet owes something to Japanese art, which had just come into fashion. In evidence, too, is his propensity for binding forms with firm and continuous contour-lines, at once synthetic and flowing with unruffled ease. For the time being he deserts his usual practice of inserting softly modulated transitional passages between the bright tracts of the canvas, and uses juxtaposed planes done in flat tints—which led Courbet to accuse him of making pictures that looked like playing-cards. Manet distributes on the canvas unbroken tones which tell out strongly and, thus used, suggest volumes. Also in this picture he invents a new perspective: a conception of the third dimension which was to have a lasting influence on Degas, Lautrec and Gauguin in particular and, later, on Matisse and the Fauve painters.*

ÉDOUARD MANET (1832-1883).
THE FIFER, 1866. (23 ½ × 38 ½")
LOUVRE, PARIS.

1947

EDOUARD MANET (1832-1883). LE DÉJEUNER DANS L'ATELIER, 1868-1869. (47¼ × 69″) NEUE STAATSGALERIE, MUNICH.

IN MANET'S Déjeuner, *painted in 1868, Courbet's influence is manifest. He painted his* Déjeuner *in his Paris studio, two years after Renoir's. The figures have an amazing lifelikeness; here, as always, Manet does not trouble himself with psychology, all he asks is that his figures shall be alive. Another touch of realism is the delightful still life of the oysters and the peeled lemon on the table; it has the realistic illusionism of the 17th-century Flemish and French masters of the* genre, *and, added to this, that originality in the use of color which characterizes Manet's art from beginning to end, an art four-square and flawless in its color and texture. Equally characteristic is the boldness with which Manet has placed his central figure well in the foreground exposing him to our gaze almost pitilessly, we might say. And this dark patch harmonizes so well with the rest that it avoids giving the effect of a hole bored in the canvas.*

RENOIR was twenty-five when he painted this work. He had yet to discover the true bearing of the inspiration within him. Among the most important influences affecting him were Manet (who painted his Fifer in this same year) and Courbet. That of the latter is most apparent in his Cabaret de la Mère Anthony; though Renoir sometimes referred to Courbet as "a bore," he respected him as a representative of tradition. Renoir has here painted himself in company with his friends. Lying on the table in the foreground is L'Evénement; this is the first time a newspaper is pictorially treated as an element of a still life. Shown with Renoir are Lecœur the painter, Sisley and the servant, Nana; in the background is Mère Anthony, the owner of the tavern. The back wall is covered with graffiti and daubs made by the artists or passing guests. The figure we see roughly sketched (high up, on the right) is Henri Mürger, author of La Vie de Bohème; it was done by Renoir. Though he did not think much of this canvas as a work of art, he had much affection for it because it reminded him of his Barbizon days, which he always looked back on with fond remembrance. It has no pretense to realism, no illusionist tricks are employed, and Renoir gave free rein to his penchant for bright colors.

AUGUSTE RENOIR (1841-1919). LE CABARET DE LA MÈRE ANTHONY, 1865. (77 × 51″) NATIONAL MUSEUM, STOCKHOLM.

hankered after the elegant sensuality of the 18th century. Here, even more boldly stated than before, were those superimposed planes of bright, contrasting colors, which Manet carried a stage further the following year in his *Fifer* (see Plate), also rejected by the Salon, which prompted Courbet's contemptuous remark that a picture should not be a "playing-card." A new world of painting was coming into existence, but no one as yet perceived this. At bottom, what incensed the Academy (true instigator, needless to say, of the attacks launched against Manet) was the sudden emergence of a technique that played havoc with tradition. In *The Fifer* Manet struck out for himself, and rendered real light, the light of nature, without resorting to the conventional procedure of somber oppositions, which only resulted in the quite unconvincing lighting we see in those "black, rubbed out and dirty canvases" derided by Constable. As he himself put it: "See that you have full light, full shades, all the rest will come naturally; it often amounts to very little."

It was while he was working out this technique that Manet became friendly with the Impressionists. He did not always share their views—especially that of Monet when he told him to discard the "black" of which he was so fond. At heart he was far from being a revolutionary and to make a deliberate break with tradition was the last thing he wanted.

No doubt he was influenced by Japanese art. Parisians made acquaintance with it in 1862, in that famous shop in the Arcades of the rue de Rivoli, run by Mme Soye whose husband had been to Japan. It had been on view again in 1867 at the Oriental Pavilion of the World's Fair and the vogue for all things Japanese rapidly spread. Utamaro, Hokusai and Hiroshige became familiar names and in a very short while a Japanese influence began to creep not only into Manet's work, but also into that of Monet, Degas, Gauguin, Van Gogh and Toulouse-Lautrec. All these artists had been vastly impressed by this novel, two-dimensional composition, whose impact on 19th- and 20th-century art was to be so great; also the color put on without modeling, involving an entirely new conception of perspective. Japanese aesthetic tallied, moreover, with Manet's predilection for light colors and 'blacks,' and with his way of 'insetting' forms. But while he certainly took over some Japanese procedures, this was only after carefully testing them out and adjusting them to the requirements of his very personal genius, as he always did when taking leaves from other masters' books.

Manet's great discovery, we may say, lay in ceasing to treat form as the necessary framework and color as a filling-up. In his well-known 'playing-card' method, he utilized, as we have said, the juxtaposition of light tones without transitional passages. Thus form was stripped down to essentials and broken up, and modeling by light tended to disappear in his work. Manet stood for the principle of a purely optical reality. He loathed any kind of system, even an impressionist one; the personal response was all that mattered. He sought to render in painting solely what he saw in nature, pure tonal relations sufficient in themselves for giving the effect of space. He stood out against rounding off figures in the classical manner, and practiced that method of painting in flat colors which imparts a new perspective to the composition.

THE REALISM OF DEGAS

Degas' place in 19th-century art is a peculiar one. Something of an eccentric, he was a constant source of amazement to his friends and fellow-painters, as much for the sterling qualities of his art as for his stubborn opposition to nearly all the trends of his day. Amongst the impressionist pioneers, he deliberately chose to act the part of "an old, incorrigible reactionary," as he himself described it. He was born in Paris in 1834 of a wealthy family of bankers who had frequent contacts with well-known art-collectors. Throwing up his law studies at an early age, he resolved to devote himself exclusively to painting and by the time he was twenty was already an assiduous visitor to the Louvre. After a brief period at the Ecole des Beaux-Arts, he made a trip to Italy. Upon his return he spent some time painting historical subjects. Then, striking up a friendship with Manet, he turned to portraits, pictures of the theater, dancers, horse-racing and, above all, the female body. It was he and Manet who 'discovered' Japanese art.

His own face (which he painted many times) is not a likable one; it suggests a fault-finding, cantankerous, even cruel character. He had little use for his fellow-men, nor for women either, and remained a bachelor all his life, dying nearly blind, though not without having enjoyed the most successful of careers. Degas was alert, quickwitted and a shrewd observer. The comments he made on his contemporaries are often scathing, even malignant, but invariably hit the mark. Nothing escaped his shrewd eye and alert mind. Entirely lacking in poetic imagination, he had but one aim in view: to wrest its secrets from a world of reality which obsessed him, and which he observed and analysed with a bitter pessimism whose origin remains a mystery. Guided by his precise, even finical intelligence, he laid out his flawless compositions, inspired, as often as not, by the most realistic subjects. Thus it was that he treated women's bodies so often, and always with a sort of smoldering resentment. In the rhythmic distortions he imparted to them, he attained a realism whose sweep and dynamism compel admiration. His drawing, vivid, telling, accurate, is like an instrument on which he plays a suite of variations which, despite occasional flights of rhythmic eloquence, always remain very realistic in effect. The composition is fresh and bold. Degas breaks with classical form, lowering the horizon line, using a system of vertical axes borrowed from the Japanese, foreshortening the subject as if he were wearing blinkers, or as a camera lens would do. He had no interest in colors as such; he enclosed them within the drawing, despite the contrary methods coming into vogue. He disliked Impressionism, though he was sometimes influenced by it, against his will. He had no interest in landscape either; and if he painted a few seascapes—and very fine ones they are—this must have been because he had nothing better to do at the moment.

His unconcealed contempt for color was probably due to his aversion for Impressionism; the fact is that he could and did produce canvases in which color is handled with a sensitivity and discernment that rank them beside the best works of the period. Indeed towards the end of his career, we find Degas developing into a quite amazing colorist. Flinging himself into the fray with characteristic zest, he invented a mixture of oils and pastel whose harsh and scintillating effects were an entirely new departure in art. This he slashed on with a sort of inspired frenzy, and there is no denying that the effect is startling and not devoid of grandeur.

EDGAR DEGAS (1834-1917). THE WOMAN WITH THE CHRYSANTHEMUMS, 1865. (30 × 36½″) METROPOLITAN MUSEUM OF ART, NEW YORK.

Degas never cared much for flowers; indeed, when dining with friends, he insisted on their being removed from the table. This picture is obviously due to a sudden caprice, or a challenge he had set himself. Nothing if not keen-witted, he had no illusions as to the triteness of such a subject, a conventional vase on a table—even if the vase was stacked with flowers—on which, incidentally, he lavishes a wealth of colors uncommon in his art. But he did not hesitate to break with all the precedents of classical composition, by placing just beside the vase a woman's face, sharply delineated in the Japanese manner, whose linear relations are co-ordinated plastically with the vertical lines of the vaguely stated door that forms the background of the canvas on the right.

HARMONIES OF WHISTLER

James Abbott McNeill Whistler was born on July 10, 1834, at Lowell, Massachusetts. His father, after serving as an officer in the United States Army, took up engineering and in 1842 was given an important post in the first Russian railway then under construction between Moscow and St Petersburg. Thus Whistler had an early introduction to European culture (he spent a year in England with his half-sister Mrs Haden) and moreover learnt to speak French fluently. On the death of his father (1849) the family returned to the United States. In 1851 Whistler entered the West Point Military Academy, but a military career was clearly not for him and he left after two years. He had shown a precocious aptitude for drawing and now took up a post in the Coast Survey Department, where it was thought his gift might help him on. But his topographical studies were too 'artistic' to please his superiors and anyhow his heart was not in map-making. In 1855 he achieved his secret ambition of becoming an art-student in Paris. None plunged more enthusiastically than this young American into the *Vie de Bohème* so picturesquely described by Mürger. Speaking of Whistler in this youthful phase, Théodore Duret, the famous French critic who knew him well and whose portrait (Metropolitan Museum of Art) he painted in 1883, remarked on "his habit of a separate pose, whimsical attire, a way of despising and setting at defiance the 'vulgar herd' incapable of seeing and feeling like an artist. This combination of the distinctive characteristics of a French art student and the manner of an American gentleman, in a man otherwise full of life, spirit and individuality, made of Whistler a quaint original who could not fail to be remarked everywhere."

But young Whistler, for all his eccentricities, took his art with high seriousness and worked hard as well as amusing himself. It was in the fifties that the taste for Japanese art, hitherto almost unknown, which had so strong an influence on Manet and the younger men of the period, developed in Paris. So far Whistler had been under the spell of Velazquez and his first major work, *At the Piano*, shows the Spanish master's influence, though the way the pictures hanging on the wall are treated, only the bottom strips being visible, is distinctly Whistlerian. Also, he already showed a tendency to paint in flat planes and to employ a range of low-pitched tones. Whistler had an extraordinarily versatile talent, being equally at home in oil, watercolor, lithography and etching, and in the sixties he produced a number of etchings including the famous 'Thames Set,' in which, as in the Venetian series (made in the 'eighties), he shows "a mastery considered second only to Rembrandt's" (Sheldon Cheney). Japanese influence is more or less pronounced in the paintings made in London between 1860 and 1870, which include *The Little White Girl*, *La Princesse du Pays de la Porcelaine* (1865 Salon) and *The Golden Screen* (1864).

Financial disaster befell Whistler when he brought his famous libel action against John Ruskin who in *Fors Clavigera* concluded a tirade as offensive as it was absurd with the remark that he "never expected to hear a coxcomb ask two hundred guineas

1950

—   —

While it is obvious that the composition of this work draws its inspiration, in a general way, from Japanese art, the artist has treated it in a very personal manner. The background, painted in flat tints, conforms to the Japanese notion of two-dimensional portrayal. But the woman's body is modeled on thoroughly classical lines, and her garments are rich in decorative elements, in which Whistler's delicate feeling for color is given play.

for flinging a pot of paint in the public's face.'' (It is odd that Ruskin failed to remember that the same phrase had been used some forty years earlier in criticizing a sunset by Turner, whose art he [Ruskin] had so strenuously championed.) In the trial Whistler defended his position with wit and dignity. Thus, when the opposing counsel said, "The labor of two days, then, is that for which you ask two hundred guineas?" Whistler retorted "No. I ask it for the knowledge of a lifetime." Technically he won the case, but he was ordered to pay his own costs, with the result that he was made bankrupt and all his belongings were sold. Fortunately he had his etching to fall back on. In 1879 he went to Venice and his Venetian etchings, though attacked by the critics, found a good market with connoisseurs. Gradually the tide turned in his favor, his *Portrait of the Artist's Mother* was given a medal at the Paris Salon of 1883 and later was bought by the French Government for the Luxembourg. And in the 1884 Salon his *Miss Alexander* was highly praised. Belated recognition came to him in England, too, and in 1886 he was elected President of the Royal Society of British Artists. But two years later he was forced by a hostile clique to resign, and was followed by many of the best artists of the group. Whistler's remark on this occasion was characteristic: "It's quite simple; the artists have left and the British remain." He was a brilliant writer, indeed, *The Gentle Art of making Enemies* (1890) is one of the wittiest of the many witty books published during that golden age of the 'nineties.

"All art constantly aspires to the condition of music." Walter Pater's famous dictum, which was to have so much effect on the aesthetic movement of the close of the century, is to be found in the Giorgione essay (1877) of *The Renaissance*. Though the name is not mentioned, it is difficult to believe that Pater had not Whistler in mind as well as Giorgione when he wrote these words. The titles Whistler gave his works, *Symphony in White No. 1* (originally named *The White Girl*), *Harmony in Grey and Green (Portrait of Miss Alexander)*, the many *Arrangements* and *Nocturnes* may well have come to Pater's notice. And in his *Ten O'Clock* Whistler wrote: "Nature indeed contains the elements in color and form of all pictures, as the keyboard contains the notes of all music. But the artist is born to pick and choose and group with science these elements, that the result may be beautiful—as the musician gathers his notes and forms chords, until he brings forth from chaos glorious harmonies." This "condition of music" is the antithesis of realism; music does not seek to tell a story, any more than to point a moral or to inculcate a message. Its aim is the pleasure of the ear, as exactly as that of Whistler's art is the pleasure of the eye. (It is perhaps curious that Whistler, who owed so much to the encouragement of Courbet, should have turned his back so resolutely on realism.) Thus in the *Nocturne, Southampton Water*, "modeling, structure, and form are all suppressed in the pursuit of a color harmony that suggests the beauty, poetry, and mystery of a moonlight scene in Southampton harbor" (*Art through the Ages*, Helen Gardner A. M.). No doubt Whistler's work is decorative, but we must not forget that the Renaissance frescos were also styled "decorations," and decorative design is one of the keynotes of modern art.

One of the reasons why Whistler is still regarded in some circles as a minor artist is that in his 'arrangements' no place is given to stridency, and his art has a repose, a delicate refinement out of keeping with the boisterous age we live in. In the nomenclature of his pictures Whistler himself invited comparison with music and it is perhaps in Debussy—in, for example, the *Nocturnes* and notably that exquisite *Nuages*, with their touches of Far-Eastern exoticism, their faintly sophisticated harmonies and delicacy of statement—rather than in the work of any other painter that we find echoes of the art of this great American expatriate.

SUNLIGHT AND SEALIGHT

Obsessed as they were with the idea of rendering light, neither the realist nor the romantic landscapists confined themselves to subjects to be found on land alone. Woods, fields and hills were, it is true, the natural background of their dreams of light, but actually they served rather to concentrate light, to impede its flow, even to blur it sometimes—though often, it had to be admitted, with the happiest poetic effects. Only when painters turned to observing the sea with a more attentive eye than that of the classical painters did they become aware of the amazingly increased power and brilliance light acquires when it strikes on the vast mirror of the sea. Under the boundless vault of sky, the towering cloud mountains, and gazing at the 'innumerable laughter' of the waves, they discovered some of the secrets of light in its purest, most living state. For it was here, between the expanse of sky and sea, that light enjoyed its utmost, most exultant freedom.

As it so happened, the artists picked on the very towns on the Channel coast that were soon to become the favorite resorts of fashionable society.

In the heyday of Romanticism Delacroix, Huet, Bonington and many English artists had stayed on the coast at one time or another. Then Millet had "consulted" the sea from the top of *Gréville Cliff*, near his native village of Gruchy, not far from Cherbourg. At the same time, Corot, Daubigny and Jongkind, each in turn, had roamed the coast and found many a site to their liking. Finally a whole group of artists settled at Honfleur, on the Seine estuary. It was here that Courbet met Boudin and Baudelaire, at the Ferme Saint-Siméon, La Mère Toutain's famous inn. Monet, Sisley and Bazille joined them and Jongkind

JONGKIND (1819-1891). THE HARBOR AT HONFLEUR, 1864. (9 × 12″) LOUVRE, PARIS.

That Jongkind is reckoned one of the immediate forerunners of Impressionism is due to his scenes of Dutch harbors and canals and the Normandy beaches, pictures riddled with tiny brushstrokes that cause the tones to coruscate. It is due also to his rapidly made landscape sketches, touched up with watercolors and permeated with subtle light.

1952

Courbet always scoffed at that brand of Romanticism which springs from an unbridled fancy, dealing in exotic and mythological scenes of an unlikely kind. Here, in contrast to this, we have the Courbet who all his life was enamored of power and grandeur. His temperament shines through in this well-knit work in which sea, shore and boat form a compact and sober foreground, a kind of springboard whence the eye is carried into a vast sky where storm-clouds gather.

also put in a stay there. The group came to be known as the 'Saint-Siméon School' and the artists set up their easels in the neighboring towns of Etretat, Sainte-Adresse, Le Havre, Dieppe, Varengeville and Fécamp—where Monet tried to commit suicide. Renoir, too, made stays at Pourville and Berneval. As for Manet, for whom the sea was of course nothing new, he spent a summer at Boulogne and another at Berck, but preferred Cherbourg where, in 1864, he is said to have witnessed the sea-fight between two American men-of-war, the *Kearsarge* and the *Alabama*, of which he made a large picture (now in the Philadelphia Museum of Art).

Thus there was nothing short of a migration of artists to the Channel beaches, especially between 1858, when Boudin and Jongkind met for the first time, and about 1870, when Impressionism reached its peak with the 'Argenteuil Period' and the return of the painters to the outlying districts west of Paris.

CLAUDE MONET (1840-1926). THE BEACH AT SAINTE-ADRESSE, 1867. (22 ¼ × 32 ¼")
ART INSTITUTE, CHICAGO.

During the last months of 1866, in the period of his worst material difficulties, Monet stayed at Sainte-Adresse on the Channel coast. It was there that he met Manet. But there was not as yet any question of tackling the aesthetic and technical problems of Impressionism. This picture still betrays the influence of Manet and, still more so, that of Courbet, who was giving the artist many useful pointers at the time.

CAMILLE COROT (1796-1875). ROCKS ON THE SEASHORE, 1870. (39½ × 3″) MESDAG MUSEUM, THE HAGUE.

Unlike Courbet, Corot was seldom attracted by the sea and his only pictures of it, done at Venice and La Rochelle, show it locked in by quays and jetties. Thus this picture, a quite unusual one in his output, is of interest as being an attempt by Corot faithfully to render the misted light of the beaches, as his juniors, Courbet and Monet, were subsequently to do.

Corot, when painting *Yport Cliff*, did not make any attempt to bring out the distinctive features of the sea, as did Boudin, Jongkind and Monet. His seascapes are done on the same lines as his rural landscapes. His rendering of light and its gleams on water retains his fondness for delicately muted tones, in which subtle tints of grey express the 'thrill' he always felt before his subject. He refused to let himself be carried away by immediate reality, and here too re-created it with that light, intuitively fleeting touch that answers to the term 'impression,' which he was the first to use. After the classic manner, he paid no attention to the distinctive characteristics of the sea,

Northern or Mediterranean, but painted it with the same palette as he used for his Italian landscapes.

Courbet did much the same. Always he 'saw big,' and for him the sea was a heaven-sent opportunity for bodying forth his 'gigantism.' He felt at home with those endless horizons under the sky's immensity, with the majestic sea, the huge billows and giant rocks, all of which he interpreted in accordance with the promptings of his unruly temperament. Far from looking at them closely, he heightened the general effect of his seascapes by swamping all detail in the amazing range of startling hues so characteristic of his palette.

It was Jongkind and Boudin who were the first to analyse the nature of the light that plays upon the Channel.

Jongkind was born at Latrop, Holland, in 1819, the same year as Courbet. He came to Paris in 1845 and, after spending several years in Rotterdam, returned to France for good, dying there in 1891. He was a sick man and found in alcohol the

EUGÈNE BOUDIN (1824-1898). A NORMANDY BEACH, 1881. (8 × 14½″) PRIVATE COLLECTION, PARIS.

If Boudin has been regarded as one of the inspirers of Impressionism, it was because of the particular attention he gave to the problems of light, which were to become one of the leading interests of that school. It was Boudin, too, who discovered Monet and disclosed new horizons in painting to him. Boudin's beach scenes deserved their popularity; coruscating with broken lights, they combine most skillful artistry with charm.

consolations that he sought in vain elsewhere. Always haunted by persecution mania, he ended his days in an insane asylum. For him nature was a refuge, a haven of calm and light, serenity and safety. Lacking any culture, artistic or other, he had no mind for books or discussions on art. Of Courbet, who inflicted his realist theories on him, he said: "His claptrap just bores me." For him, the appeal of the sea did not consist in the storms and billows dear to Courbet, but in the serene, limitless expanse of water, the vastness of the sky with its gently undulating clouds. He enjoyed languid curves, and likewise the long, calm lines of canals and roads, the sense of restfulness that flows from horizontals of all kinds. When, in depicting vast expanses, he strewed his canvas with tiny juxtaposed touches, this was never for purely technical reasons; it was thus he could express the light that freed him from his inhibitions, and satisfy his craving for breathing space in which his sensitivity, fretted to a breaking-point by over-indulgence in drink and physical suffering, could find alleviation. At heart, he had no special fondness for the sea. Always a prey to irrational impulses, which took his friends by surprise, Jongkind was a man apart, incalculable. Monet, however, who made friends with him, valued his advice and called him "the only good painter of seascapes." Jongkind was a thorough-going exponent of that mystico-romantic ideal, the complete fusion of Nature and the artist's Ego. And though he is numbered among the precursors of Impressionism —primarily because of this ideal, and also for his technical innovations—he was really one of those who overshot the limits of the movement before it had even begun, giving as he did free rein to his tendency towards intense emotional expression.

We may say of Jongkind's art that it is "impressionist" by anticipation, whereas Boudin's is already "Impressionism." Boudin was born at Honfleur in 1824 and died at Deauville in 1898, after living most of his life on the Channel coast. The sea meant much to him, but he viewed it with a painter's eye exclusively, whereas Jongkind used it as a means to self-expression. In fact Boudin saw the sea in terms of 'seascapes.' With something of the artisan in him, as orderly and level-headed as Jongkind was highly strung, he calmly analysed his raw material, the beaches, with almost the precision of a scientist. Exquisitely composed, if perhaps a trifle over-precious and showy, his palette sedulously rendered each detail of sea and harbor, but no true feeling for nature is apparent in the kaleidoscopic patterns of his color. In his pictures the clashes of light between sky and sea, white skirts on the beaches and the white forms of clouds played off against one another, produce delicate, unexpected effects. He aimed at registering the impression of the fleeting hour, and did it marvelously well. Boudin had the simplicity of a Sunday painter eager to note down everything in sight, an attitude not lost on the Impressionists, especially on Monet who, in later years, credited Boudin with having "opened his eyes."

Monet was born in 1840 in Paris, but spent his childhood at Le Havre, on the Channel coast, beside the ships and the sea; water had a constant fascination for his keen, discerning eye, and he sought to plumb the secrets of its glittering surfaces and mysterious depths, not only in the Channel and the North Sea, but also in the Mediterranean, the Adriatic, and the Atlantic—not to mention any number of streams, rivers and even ponds. It was water that suggested to him the prismatic breaking-up of light and color, which resulted in a heightened sense of sight, opening fields of inquiry hitherto undreamed-of. The impressionist revolution was set on foot by Monet, who evolved the new methods called for, the division of tones, chromatism, the suppression of local color—and all this in the course of a ceaseless study of the play of light on water and its refractions. Indeed, apart from their prodigious technique, his interpretations of the Channel beaches constitute a record almost analytic in its nature; we are amazed at Monet's uncanny power of capturing every feature of the sea's face, and the very soul of water under all its changing aspects.

We should note at this point that it was Corot who first used the word 'impression' in connection with painting, while 'impressionism' was coined by a journalist ridiculing a picture by Monet, entitled *Sunrise: Impression.*

It has been suggested that the origin of Impressionism, in the form in which we find it round about 1870, was a reaction against Academicism, or against both Romanticism and Realism. This theory, put forward by many art-critics, though plausible, seems beside the mark. Actually, Impressionism was primarily a carrying of realist doctrines to their extreme conclusion, and, secondly, a new way of looking at reality, sponsored by a small number of artists gifted with exceptionally keen eyesight. Thanks to this gift, they discovered new relationships between colors and applied to these an optical chemistry of their own devising. Some of the impressionist aims and methods date back of course to an older day: the breaking up of tones, the use of complementary colors, the attempt to render the true light of day. Here we might draw up a sort of 'honors list' of forerunners in which would be included, amongst others, Pintoricchio, Van der Weyden, Claude Lorrain, Chardin, Constable, Turner, Delacroix, and finally Jongkind and Boudin. Yet, however true it is that the credit for a discovery is never due to one man only and that the ingredients of Impressionism were not wholly new, there is no denying that the Impressionists gave a new direction to the art of the period.

Impressionism, then, put forward a new way of viewing reality: all living things are in a continuous process of change and if life is to be seen as it really is, it must be broken down and expressed in its fleeting, transitory states. We need only recall the observations of Constable and Chateaubriand on the changes nature undergoes in the course of the hours, or the old saying of Heraclitus: "Everything is flowing. You cannot step into the same river twice." Bringing new methods to bear, the Impressionists attempted to fix on canvas the momentary aspects of nature's ever-changing scenes, reconstituted with almost scientific precision. And so for a time the pantheistic view of nature was forgotten, but it came back again when the artists, seeing their technical experiments crowned with success, gave free rein to the expression of their sensations. At the start, however, with the groundwork still being laid and the Impressionists-to-be still groping for their path, they lacked that overall view of the movement through which its technical methods could be ordered and clarified. With the young revolution in full swing, given the inevitable cross-purposes of its pioneers, no one could say what

CLAUDE MONET (1840-1926). SAILING BOAT AT ARGENTEUIL, C. 1873. (30 × 22″) F. W. BRAVINGTON COLLECTION, HENLEY-ON-THAMES.

Done in broad, slashing strokes, this picture dates from that period when, within a few short years, the Impressionist conception of landscape had come into its own. Monet, working at Argenteuil, then at Vétheuil, set out to record the subtly changing, evanescent effects of light and its sudden gleams on water. Only later, at Giverny, Belle-Ile and Antibes, did he indulge in color with the rapturous abandon we find in his famous 'series,' especially in that of the *Waterlilies*.

ultimately it would lead to. The most immediate needs were dealt with and, with no thought for the morrow, the old was torn down and the new set up in makeshift fashion, to be changed later on or perfected, as the case might be. Thus an impressionist procedure gradually took form, and matured into an homogenous whole; until a day came when Cézanne announced his intention of making Impressionism "solid and abiding, like the old masters." As the data of observation were sorted out, the mechanics of the Impressionist technique came into being: division and juxtaposition of tones, the association of

With the exception of a few painting trips to Rouen, Dieppe and Paris, Pissarro worked almost entirely at Pontoise, Louveciennes and Eragny. Unlike Monet and Sisley, in whose landscapes the human figure played a subordinate role, Pissarro recorded the life of the peasants, at work in the fields or amusing themselves at country-fairs. His art, less poetic than Monet's, more robust than Sisley's, is exceptional for the accuracy and variety of its color, for the deep communion with nature that it reveals, and for a tectonic sense unusual in Impressionism, preoccupied as were the other artists with the rendering of fugitive, atmospheric effects.

complementary colors, a more thorough-going use of values, and the abolishing of local color, which is a mere construction of the mind. Black was now regarded as a color, and light was split up prismwise; sunlight was regarded as the sole source of color, and color as in itself capable of creating form and contour.

The influence of the movement was nothing short of worldwide; it still persists and is destined to endure. For after Impressionism, painting could never again be what it was before—not only because of the new outlook on the world to which it had given rise, but because its discoveries were essentially technical and sensorial.

Impressionism really begins with Claude Monet (1840-1926), for he was the leader-to-be of the movement. At the start, as was only natural, he followed the footsteps of his immediate predecessors and took over the tonalities of Corot and Courbet. But it was he who in the end swung Manet, Renoir, Pissarro and Sisley around to his personal views, and this amid unremitting hard work, extreme financial straits and violent disapprobation. With a courage that forces our admiration, Monet stood by his theories, and saw them through to the end regardless of the others' deviations. He is the heroic figure in Impressionism, for he carried its principles to their logical conclusion, perfecting his analyses of light with unremitting zeal and thoroughness. At the end of his career he painted his famous 'series': cathedrals, haystacks, poplars and, above all, waterlilies. In them the subject itself is reduced to the state of a vague sketch, a mere suggestion, little heed being paid to composition and drawing. In a visionary ecstasy the artist painted solely in patches and gleams, 'reflections of reflections,' evanescent nuances refined almost to the point of abstraction. Perhaps, in the light of the syntheses that Renoir and Cézanne achieved, there seems to have been something over-analytical in Monet's approach to art. Yet all new trends in art take their rise from a moving spirit with a more or less cut-and-dried program, and the moving spirit

in this case was obviously Monet, whose greatness lies in his having stood out so obstinately against the concessions and vagaries of the others, notably of Pissarro.

The personality of Camille Pissarro (1830-1903) had not the same compelling force as Monet's. He selected from the impressionist technique just those elements which were to lead him to a more classical and, at the same time, more human conception of art. For he was the link between Impressionism and tradition and the trend he gave his art had a fruitful influence on Cézanne. Pissarro was a builder; he mistrusted those fugitive effects which were the speciality of Impressionism. He lacked the bold vision of Monet and it was only after watching his friends at work in the

ALFRED SISLEY (1839-1899). LA ROUTE DE LA PRINCESSE A LOUVECIENNES, 1875. DURAND-RUEL COLLECTION, PARIS.

The hall-mark of Sisley's art is a serene and delicate tenderness. We must not look to him for the ardor of Monet, the tectonic composition of Pissarro or the sensuality of Renoir. With spontaneous ease and elegance, never indulging in irrelevant effects, he sings of hours and days that drift away, a song fresh and poetic, often with undertones of melancholy.

1959

—   —

EDOUARD MANET (1832-1883). SAILING, C. 1874. (38 × 51 ½″) METROPOLITAN MUSEUM OF ART,
NEW YORK.

Shortly after 1870, Manet, much taken by the fresh, original style of his junior, Monet, abandoned his earlier manner. In such pictures as *Argenteuil, Le Cabaret du Père Lathuile* and *Washing-day,* he employed a palette of intense tones and attempted, by using a multiplicity of touches, to render the brightness of colors in the full light of day.

open air that he too set up his easel in front of the subject. He was especially fond of broad planes, monuments, five-storey houses, towers, rivers, and roads; when he did figures they usually filled up most of the picture. The coruscations of impressionist color were never sought for by Pissarro. His admiration went first to Millet and Corot, and the most personal, emotionally convincing of his pictures depict the life of country-folk, fields, orchards, and woodlands. His indifference to the fugacity of time is manifest in his essentially static compositions, where movement is never more than latent in the serene, stately attitudes of his peasants. It is in his work, moreover, that we find that renewal of classical form, to which revolutionary painters invariably have recourse when they realize the need for the abiding qualities indispensable to the balanced work of art.

Alfred Sisley (1839-1899) cuts the figure of an aristocrat out of his element amongst the pioneers whose work he so much admired. Born in Paris of a fairly well-to-do English family, he received an excellent schooling. It was almost with misgivings that he threw in his lot with Monet and Renoir, whose ideas he found a little too daring for his taste. He, too, followed in Corot's footsteps. He had the same natural gentleness, the same delicate feeling for all the smiling, intimate, simple things of nature. Towering cliffs, raging seas, forests and gigantic cloud-formations were to him cumbersome subjects, and he ruled them out. He preferred the countryside of the Ile-de-France, whose restrained harmonies he expressed with a palette which was certainly impressionist in range, but which he never handled with the intransigence of the other members of the group. Though he was often desperately hard-up, we do not find the least trace of bitterness or dejection in his paintings of Argenteuil, Saint-Germain, Moret and the banks of the Loing. He added a touch of romance to nature, and a smiling grace, but without a shade of affectation.

We have seen how great was Manet's importance as a pathfinder. His influence carried over beyond Impressionism, whose shortcomings are evident in the light of his work. His knowledge of, and reverence for, the art of the past, combined with his natural discretion and prudence, warned him off all that seemed unduly novel and had not stood the test of time. He did not care for painting in the open, nor would he discard his 'blacks,' whose contrast values he considered indispensable. Manet was not interested in 'fixing' the fugitive moment; he preferred the permanent and classical. To be sure, his quickness of mind kept him abreast of the new experiments, the more so as he was a born painter, keenly responsive to any new ideas on the rendering of light, regardless of the methods involved. But Manet made no actual contribution to the impressionist movement and his personal contacts with its members found no echo in his art. Yet we must do him credit for sharing their passion for light and indulging it with great success, if along the lines of the contrasts used in classical painting.

Under its outward aspect of voluptuous hedonism, Renoir's art, like that of several nineteenth-century masters, conceals a very human drama, from his beginnings under the influence of the great men of the previous generation, down to his last phase, in which all the appearances of reality merge in the Dionysian rapture of his light. His admiration was shared between Ingres and Courbet in equal measure. With him the antinomy of reason and instinct was never reconciled; thus we often find him talking of his 'research-work'—an indication of his continually hesitant state of mind. "In 1883," he said, "there was a sort of break in my work." Under the influence of Ingres, he was then passing through what he called his 'harsh' period, of which one of his contemporaries said: "These Renoirs are sour fruit that will never ripen." But what was the real object of his "research"?

We must remember that he had a difficult start in life. He was born at Limoges in 1841. His father was a small tailor with seven children to support. The family moved to Paris when young Renoir was four years old and he was soon sent off to grammar school. His schooling never got beyond this stage. But he was a quick-witted boy, and to his natural intelligence was due his faculty for acquiring knowledge of all kinds, and

AUGUSTE RENOIR (1841-1919). WOMAN IN A BOAT, 1877. (28¾ × 35″) ALBERT LASKER COLLECTION, NEW YORK.

Between 1860 and 1880 boating on the Seine was a popular pastime with the young people of Paris. In many of his short stories Maupassant has described those carefree days out of doors. Renoir took up this theme at the same time, sketching and painting the groups of young men and women enjoying their outings on the water. For him it was an excellent opportunity for extolling woman's beauty in the brilliant light of the summer sun.

developing his talents to the utmost. At thirteen he was sent to work in a china factory, where he was employed on painting decorative designs on dishware; then on fans, blinds and the like. In his leisure moments, which were few, he visited the Louvre, where he was much impressed by Boucher. At sixteen he did a portrait of his grandmother, his first known work. At twenty he entered the Ecole des Beaux-Arts where he made the acquaintance of Monet, Sisley and Bazille. Several years went by, and then he met Diaz at Barbizon. At last, in 1865, he exhibited a portrait and a landscape at the Salon, and this was the starting-point of a long, brilliant career.

Renoir had a slender, elegant figure, and the refined sensuality of his face was stressed by large eyes sparkling with intelligence. He wore a beard, that necessary embellishment of painters in his day; but his, like Manet's, was well trimmed and cared for, very different from the bushy, unkempt beards that were the peculiar pride of the Barbizon painters. The key to his nature was an acute sensitivity allied with cautious reserve; to these he gave expression in his conversation and his observations on art, always very much to the point, but sometimes hinting at divided purposes. He had no compunctions about traversing the opinions and tendencies of his contemporaries. Much was then being said of the identification of man with nature, but Renoir, for his part, balked at any meek submission to emotions inspired by nature. It was a momentous turning-point for nineteenth-century painting when Renoir, as against Millet, Corot, Courbet and Monet, declared that it is not by looking at nature that a man learns to paint, but by looking at the masterpieces in museums. This bold statement was nothing short of a challenge to the Zeitgeist; intellect was by way of taking its revenge on instinct. It is all the more surprising coming from him, an artist driven on by compelling instinctual forces which the rudimentary education he had received seemed little qualified to check. But his natural shrewdness warned him that painting cannot dispense with certain laws of construction. The study of the aspects of nature, the rendering of atmospheric changes, the close scrutiny of detail—these are means, not ends in themselves. After 'trying his hand out' at Impressionism, for example in his *Grenouillères*, he was led to mistrust the impressionist addiction to bright tones, the effect of which, to his mind, was no more than that of brilliant fireworks. At bottom it was the Venetian masters whom he loved, and, amongst moderns, Delacroix, Courbet and the Ingres of the odalisques. The firm, plastic flow of their line appealed to him. And he felt that color—which he modeled with such a light and infinitely supple hand—should always submit to the demands of form; so that his palette became almost monochrome. This led on, round about 1905, to another 'break' in his art. And now he assigned to color the role of controlling form. He let it play its leading part in perfect freedom; it became a vehicle of pure poetry, and, on the aesthetic side, the constructive, carefully controlled range of his palette brought him nearer to the art of his dreams, a sublimation of the human figure into the divine, a merging of desire and achievement in a hymn of joy, the song of praise the art of his last years indites. It was then that he exclaimed: "What splendid men those Greeks were! The earth, the Paradise of the Gods—that's what I want to paint."

'FIN DE SIÈCLE' CLIMATE

EDGAR DEGAS (1834-1917). LE CAFÉ-CONCERT DES AMBASSADEURS, 1876-1877. (14 × 10″) MUSÉE DES BEAUX-ARTS, LYONS.

The superb composition and craftsmanship of this work are disguised in the fluid ease of its execution. Degas was one of the first to take up this theme, which has become so characteristic of modern painting. Baudelaire helped it come into vogue and it has more recently found expression in the numerous clowns, dancers and harlequins of Picasso and Rouault.

The vogue of the sea-beaches had worked itself out, the secrets of sealight been explored, and now painters began to turn their attention to the gay crowd of holiday-makers. Though the costumes of the day, the multicolored parasols, shawls and furbelows were picturesque enough, the artists were not interested so much in this picturesqueness as in the possibilities they saw for new experiments in handling color. And now the scene of their activities shifted to the country districts west of Paris, to Argenteuil, Bougival, Marly, Saint-Germain, Vétheuil, the little cafés on the banks of the Seine and the Oise; to boating-parties and regattas. Next, they explored the possibilities of the Parisian scene, and found exciting subjects ready to their hand in the *bals populaires*, the Moulin de la Galette at Montmartre (which inspired first Renoir, then Lautrec), the cabarets—and especially *Le Chat Noir* and *Le Mirliton*—the open-air concerts, the cafés haunted by the artists (*Volpini, Guerbois*, the *Nouvelle Athènes*, the *Bar des Folies-Bergère* dear to Manet), the theaters, including the *Opera* and its ballet-girls, the *Cirque Fernando* and the *Nouveau Cirque* (in which Degas, Renoir and Lautrec found congenial subjects), public fairs, race-meetings, and the busy traffic of the Paris streets.

An interesting point is that in the handling of many of these scenes there is no question of painting in the open air. This was the gaslight age, and the lighting of the pictures of singers and dancers comes from footlights or 'Auer' incandescent lamps.

AUGUSTE RENOIR (1841-1919). LE MOULIN DE LA GALETTE, 1876. (45 × 30½″) LOUVRE, PARIS.

In this work we have one of Renoir's masterpieces, expressing to the full the extraordinary character of his painterly gifts and his poetic vision. Much as Watteau had done, transfiguring the antics of Italian comedians into graceful pictures, Renoir here transformed a noisy, carefree gathering of young people into a delightful medley of sparkling color in which the wide range and richness of the tones give a vivid impression of the holiday atmosphere.

PAINTING OUTSIDE FRANCE

Impressionism took some little time in making its influence felt abroad, especially in Germany. Though the idea behind Impressionism—of close communion between man and nature—was romantic enough, the scientific procedures used by the French artists in putting it into practice had little interest for the typical Germanic artist. While during the second half of the century such artists as Feuerbach (1829-1880), Hans von Marées (1837-1887) and Adolf von Menzel (1815-1905) drew their inspiration from a thoroughly romantic idealism, the technical means employed by them were always academic. What interested them was the expression of an idea; the way in which this was achieved was of secondary importance. Courbet spent some time in Germany, especially in Munich, but his stay there had no lasting effect on German art. Only one man, Wilhelm Leibl (1844-1908), Courbet's disciple, turned out some excellent realistic pictures, but they met with little success. His very realistic feeling for nature found an outlet in themes of present-day life, and in handling these he displayed complete sincerity; indeed his robust, quite unsophisticated works of this order are often more emotive than his teacher's, though they do not show the same vivacity and inventiveness in the use of color. Many of his portraits have a gentleness and discretion reminiscent of Corot.

Very different was Arnold Boecklin (1827-1906), a native of Basel who made his home in Germany. None better than he has expressed the romantic yearnings of the Germanic soul. He has a fondness for mythological scenes, which he interpreted with masterly vigor and in highly effective color. The women in his pictures, sirens, naiads and the like, remind us of Renoir at his most voluptuous. Also he painted some admirable portraits, at once firmly drawn and broadly modeled. But Boecklin's contemporary appeal is due above all to his allegories, some of which, notably the *Toteninsel*, have enjoyed worldwide fame. He was a poet and his art is essentially that of a man endowed with second sight, a visionary. Not without reason do our 20th-century Surrealists regard him as one of their precursors and for them his exuberant art is full of suggestive pointers.

In Switzerland Barthelemy Menn (1805-1893) followed up the teachings of Corot, and his work is imbued with sincerely felt emotion. While Hodler, his pupil (1853-1918), is chiefly known as a painter of vast allegorical murals, some of his smaller works are full of delicate touches and rank high in the art of the period. Coming from Belgium and settling in Paris, Alfred Stevens brilliantly delineated the elegant life of the Second Empire and the beginnings of the Third Republic. Impressionism made very slow headway in Belgium. The outstanding figure of the period was James Ensor (born in 1860) who in painting his famous *Jardin d'Amour* (in 1890) obviously paid no heed to impressionist aesthetic but went serenely ahead to create his own world of original and distinctive charms. Only in the work of Braekeleer did impressionist influence make its presence felt.

IN THE IMPRESSIONIST PERIOD

Round about 1848 a new movement took form in England. Some young men decided that the time was ripe for a campaign against the decadence and frivolities of the art of the previous century, and for a return to an aesthetic based on the unsophisticated art of the Italian Quattrocento. The painter whose art especially they singled out for attack was Lawrence, whom they accused of shallowness on the moral side, of superficial, merely showy technical adroitness and a lack of real knowledge. As against this, they made much of the ingenuousness of the Primitives, their naively faithful renderings of the human face and nature and their lofty religious ideal. To their mind, the decadence of art began with the Renaissance, of which in a general way they disapproved, and, regarding the Quattrocento as the Golden Age of painting, they aimed at re-establishing its aesthetic principles. They described themselves as Pre-Raphaelites, not so much because they had any special dislike for Raphael, as because for them he symbolized the beginning of art's decadence.

The movement was, in the last analysis, more literary than pictorial, nor did these artists impugn the technique of the Renaissance; quite otherwise, they freely borrowed from it. It was their religious instinct that rebelled against the sensuous paganism of the Renaissance masters. Against this they set up a chivalrous, romantic conception of love—a characteristically British fusion of the ideal with the real. And so they founded that famous 'Brotherhood,' which, however, like most groups of this sort, had only a few years' effective existence. With the high seriousness of neophytes they affixed to their signatures the letters P. R. B. (Pre-Raphaelite Brotherhood). Again, like most art movements, Pre-Raphaelitism had its prophet; this was John Ruskin, the eloquent champion of the great Quattrocento Florentine artists and the Cathedrals.

Son of an Italian poet living in exile in London, Dante Gabriel Rossetti (1828-1882), poet and painter, who as a boy had taken lessons from Cotman, was their moving spirit. In his *Beata Beatrix* and his *Ecce Ancilla Domini*, the atmosphere of trance-like ecstasy admirably expresses that combination of the religious and the sentimental which gives Pre-Raphaelite art its distinctive flavor. Holman Hunt (1827-1910) was a fervent Christian; his compositions have more vigor than his friends'. John Everett Millais (1829-1896) was the most painterly of the group; in his *Ophelia* and *Knight Errant* he explores new methods of rendering landscapes and faces. The art of Edward Burne-Jones (1833-1898) is still more human, more poignant. George Frederick Watts was essentially a painter of allegories, such as his famous *Hope* and *Love and Life*; here we can trace a certain filiation with Blake.

The Pre-Raphaelites were quite unaffected by the continental art of the day; they had nothing to take over from romantic, realist or impressionist techniques. All they wanted was to express their feelings with 'primitive' sincerity, and for this the purely academic procedures gave them all they needed.

In the United States we find, to begin with, in the work of George Inness (1825-1894) persistent echoes of the School of Barbizon. Presently, however, greater interest was shown in color and several painters gave it a preponderant role. Thus Winslow Homer (1836-1910) and Thomas Eakins (1844-1916) are brilliant colorists, with something of the color magic of the Spaniards and Venetians. Albert Pinkham Ryder (1847-1917), an impenitent Romantic, painted, during the impressionist period, richly colored visions, to which we shall recur; while the compositions of George Fuller (1822-1884) have a fine poetic quality. Impressionism found its exponent in Mary Cassatt (1845-1926), a sensitive, highly gifted artist, who after being influenced by Velazquez, then by Courbet, joined forces with the Impressionists, and made her home in France; in Frank Duveneck (1848-1919), who worked with Courbet's pupils at Munich; also in William Chase (1849-1916), who in 1889 succeeded in getting two of Monet's pictures accepted by the Metropolitan Museum of Art, New York—at a time when their admission to the Louvre, or even the Luxembourg Gallery, was never given a moment's consideration. Impressionist influences are visible also in the work of Theodore Robinson, Childe Hassam (1859-1935), Ernest Lawson (1875), William Glackens, John Twachtman (1853-1902), Homer Martin and Robert Loftin Newman. The prestige of the School of Barbizon was operative, too, for Paris, as Alfred H. Barr observed, has always been the chief foreign art center influencing American artists.

During the 19th century Italian art had much the same experiences as French art. And in Italy, too, the dominant factor was the artist's desire to be left completely free to express his emotions on his own lines. Round about 1858 a new School was founded at Florence (as usual in a café: in this case the 'Michelangelo') known as 'I Macchiaioli,' and in France as 'Les Tachistes,' whose procedure, as these names imply, was to paint in 'patches' or 'blobs' of color. They began their activities by a campaign against academic art, and Degas gave them his blessing. Their aim was an emotive interpretation of visual experience as it really is, without any visionary or dramatic implications à la Delacroix. This art reminds us more of the Romanticism of Corot and the School of Barbizon. Actually the name given this School is misleading; though their 'patches' exploit all the resources of color and display much boldness and originality in the individual brushstrokes, they are usually bound together by a structural lay-out and governed by a very special system of composition, and doubtless it was this that won Degas' approval. We find it in the work of Silvestro Lega (1826-1895), Signorini (1855-1901), first to exploit the 'tachisme' of Boldini (1846-1884) who became the painter of fashionable Parisian society, and especially Giovanni Fattori (1825-1908), a brilliant colorist, but also gifted with a fine sense of rhythm, who, while exalting nature, always kept very near to it.

Like the Impressionists in France, the Macchiaioli brought to Italian art some happy *trouvailles* in the spheres of color and composition. Their aesthetic fell in line with certain innovative tendencies which, generally speaking, were gaining ground in Europe and the United States.

5

THE DAWN
OF THE TWENTIETH
CENTURY

Under the auspices of Cézanne and Seurat on the one hand and Gauguin and Van Gogh on the other, the coming century was to perpetuate, but under renovated forms, the divergent trends of Classicism and Romanticism. In the art of both Cézanne and Seurat the composition of the picture is ruled by deliberate objectivity, which imposes order on the sensation and canalizes it. In the case of Gauguin and Van Gogh it is the purely subjective sensation that conditions the work and determines its structure. But in both modes of expression the great lessons of Impressionism are not lost sight of, and in both we find a complete fusion of subject and object in the composition.

CLIMAX OF THE XIXᵀᴴ CENTURY

CLAUDE MONET. ROUEN CATHEDRAL, 1894. (40 × 29″) LOUVRE, PARIS.

The artist's freedom of expressing his sensations was carried to such extremes that it ended up by running amok. The persistent breaking-up of every color into its elements and that amazing skill in ringing the changes on complementary colors displayed by Monet led to something that looked less like a picture than a sort of crazy quilt, a mix-up of all the hues of the rainbow. Colors were treated as so much raw material which called for skillful handling but signified next to nothing; they were not withheld by any boundaries, but allowed to overlap the form to which they were related. The general effect was rather like that of a roll of painted cloth.

But the spectator expects the work of art to be something more than a mere patchwork; though it need not have a documentary value, it should possess wholeness and unity; the picture should be an object having its end within itself and a life of its own, regulated by the organic laws of its being. Thus the desirability of a return to classical discipline, a sense of structure and feeling of design made itself more and more strongly felt. Monet's last works were the culmination of an aesthetic that, after its heyday during the second half of the 19th century, had lapsed into disintegration. Even so, it was in Monet that the Impressionist revolution found its most eloquent spokesman and in our eyes today he is the best example of Impressionist technique and the chief symbol of the movement.

BIRTH OF THE XXᵀᴴ CENTURY

Cézanne knew exactly what he meant when he talked of "doing Poussin again, after nature," that is to say building up within the limits of the composition the impressions he experienced when he contemplated nature. He left his sensations free to inspire the work, but only on condition that they preserved order amongst themselves. Color was the starting-off point of Cézanne's inspiration. He let the color construct the form and set the rhythm of the picture, after having carefully scrutinized the 'motif' and re-organized the data it provided.

PAUL CÉZANNE (1839-1906). LES GRANDES BAIGNEUSES, 1898-1905. (82 × 98 ½″) MUSEUM OF ART, PHILADELPHIA.

CONSTRUCTIVE FORM

Reacting against the exaggerated use of 'transitional passages' in painting, the Impressionists were led to stress color at the expense of form. It was to this state of things that Cézanne tried to provide a corrective, without, however, entirely rejecting impressionist doctrines. Thus he spoke of his desire "to make of Impressionism something solid and abiding, like the old masters." But Cézanne was a Latin. And we may be sure he had in mind no a priori blueprint of what he wanted to build, but as he went along worked out an architecture on entirely original lines. His taking-off point was Impressionism, which is to say that his inspiration derived from an immediate response, from what he liked to call his 'little sensation.' This in turn sprang from his particular way of seeing the world. The object, formerly treated as a mere ornament, later as a sort of household god, was promoted by him to the status of a microcosm, once he had thoroughly examined it 'from the life.' Despite the great variety of these little sensations, due to the swarm of impressions crowding in on him from outside, he never felt any lack of confidence. He once said: "I shall always remain the primitive of the path I have opened up," and this was literally true. But Cézanne did not go blindly down this path; his native prudence led him to apply to the impressions he received, his theories of the architectural construction of the picture. But he was committed to no predetermined system of building. Cézanne remained an impressionist in the sense that he let himself be influenced by those changeful effects of color which are often so deceptive; but instead of using them for descriptions of the fleeting moment, he employed them for gradually bringing out the essential forms of objects—a process he called 'modulating.' In order to express form by color, he strewed the canvas with a network of rhythms fanning out, complementing and balancing one another. He was fascinated by geometry and declared that "everything in nature is modeled on the lines of the cylinder, the cone and the sphere." But his chief concern was to fill his canvas with interlocking geometric planes delineated by plastic elements borrowed from the real world. Thus he worked out a new method of rendering depth, which called for a new kind of perspective. Such was the revolution effected by Cézanne's art.

With Seurat the problem of tectonic form was diverted from the organization of sensations, pre-conized by Cézanne, to the ordering of the actual picture surface. His aim was to insert three dimensions on a surface that had only two, and this by means of contrasts and analogies, without in any sense 'hollowing' the canvas. He used rhythmic curves and arabesques to evoke a new conception of space, a kind of flat perspective. Seurat progressed from the small impressionist brushstroke to the 'dot' of pointilliste art. But while the former had hitherto been used for purely analytical ends, the 'dot' in his art was an essentially constructive and synthetic factor.

It was, we may add, not without scruples and hesitation that Seurat turned back to certain classical conceptions, though he used them in a wider sense than had hitherto been customary. The effect of the Impressionist revolution in the second half of the century had been too profound even for artists classical in temperament to remain unaffected by it. And in the new fever of experiment, Seurat once went so far as to paint the frame of the picture and carry over the dots of the canvas on to the wood. He did not, however, continue this practice, but henceforth used the frame as a kind of insulator, making of the picture an object apart, a self-sufficient whole, complete in itself.

With Seurat, moreover, the problem of form was viewed from a new angle. His point of departure was a set of principles which he had arrived at himself by direct observation. With these 'laws' as a basis, he went on to infer others in the light of his own emotions, the underlying force of his unflagging experiments. With him the notion of mere representation was replaced by that of artistic experiment, an idea destined to be much exploited during the 20th century, in particular among the Fauves and Cubists.

SEURAT (1859-1890). LE
CHAHUT, 1889. (8½ ×
6½″) LONDON, THE EXE-
CUTORS OF THE LATE
SAMUEL COURTAULD.

The revelation
of a new classicism was
impending and in the
case of Seurat, involved
a swing-back to the trad-
itional notion of a pre-
determined composition.
For to Seurat sensation
was no longer a starting-
off point; he allowed it
full expression only
after having carefully
planned the structure of
his picture. He bore in
mind such doctrines of
the classical past as the
'Divine Proportion,' the
'Golden Section,' the
'Portal of Harmony'
and put them to good
use. Also, he studied
the work of scientists
like Helmholtz, Charles
Henry and Chevreul on
simultaneous contrasts
and other color theories.
Delacroix' systematic
ordering of relationships
was carried a step
further by Seurat. He
collated the classical
rules and regulated the
expression of sensations
accordingly. Some of
the Cubists took over his
aesthetic, above all his
notion of a picture no
longer the mere repre-
sentation of a fact, but a
'fact' in its own right.

THE PROBLEM OF COLOR

Cézanne aimed at interpreting what we might describe as purely optical emotions and sought no more than this; Van Gogh's and Gauguin's approach to the problems of visual experience aimed at a great deal more. Both men wished painting to express not only sensations but also personal feelings, and to reconcile the material with the spiritual; in other words, closely to fuse the form and the matter of expression. Here we have the sources of Fauvism and Expressionism, as well as the differences that were to bring these two tendencies into conflict in the 20th century.

Thus the role assigned to technique in painting acquired a new significance. The Impressionists were regarded as far too much the slaves of optical procedures, and Cézanne as too much engrossed in the architecture of forms. Line and color were now evaluated in terms of their impact on "the thinking mind," as Van Gogh and Gauguin rather pompously described it. Line and color were even called upon to interpret feeling that words fall short of expressing. Thus Van Gogh claimed to be able to express "those terrible things, men's passions" by red and green, while Gauguin maintained that line and color could define "the grandiose stature of the artist." He also asserted there were "some noble tones, some vulgar ones; some harmonies that are quiet and consoling, others whose audacity excites us" and so forth. Thus lines and colors were put to the service of a new symbolism. And just as there was a 'language of flowers,' so a language of colors now came into being. Two things were asked of painting: to please the eye by the beauty of its technical accomplishment, and to gratify the mind by its expression of the inner life. In other words, a union of content with the containing medium. Color was to play the leading part, and account was taken of its curative powers, its baleful influences and also its decorative possibilities. Under such names as Synthesism and Cloisonnism, new disciplines were imposed on it. A new symbolism of color was born, enriching its resources, broadening its vocabulary, giving its functions a new bearing. Hence it was that Gauguin was so fond of the Primitives of all times and places; for they too treated painting as a language in which they expressed their thoughts. Indeed Van Gogh and Gauguin were so literally Primitives themselves, that we find their successors, the Fauves, ignoring their theories completely —and concentrating their attention on the new techniques they introduced—much as the Renaissance painters, forgetting the faith that moved their mediaeval forerunners, devoted themselves to exploiting their heritage of technical discoveries.

In time certain of Gauguin's ideas were to have unexpected repercussions. He often spoke of "suggestion," and claimed that "painting deals more with suggesting than with describing." Perhaps Gauguin meant this in an ideological sense. Yet intuition led him to discover that, when it is distributed in terms of a surface area or degrees of intensity, color no longer builds up but merely suggests form. By attaching so much importance to dream and meditation, he meant that the artist should, so far as possible, get away from the illusory appearance of the object before him. What was wanted, to his mind, was not a literal depiction of an object, but a suggestion of its equivalent in the light of the artist's own temperament.

Thus, taking its long-awaited revenge on drawing, color now became master of its own destiny. True it is that sometimes even the best of ideas have their day and are cast aside, others taking their place. Descartes' notion of color as accident and form as truth was now literally transmuted into a new conception to which artists gave the stamp of authenticity, each marking the work of art with the 'color' of his own personality. While, in classical painting, design had controlled color, it was the latter's turn to steal a march on design, and to become henceforth the sole measure of art's integrity.

VINCENT VAN GOGH (1853-1890). THE YELLOW CORN, 1889. (28 ½ × 36″) REPRODUCED BY COURTESY OF THE TRUSTEES, TATE GALLERY, LONDON.

V<small>AN</small> G<small>OGH'S</small> *excited handling of rhythms and colors is at the opposite pole from Seurat's and Cézanne's classically ordered composition. There is no scientific theory behind his bold experiments, as there was behind those of Monet; they are of a purely sensorial order. Form and color do not serve Van Gogh as means of expressing visual experience; they enable him to exteriorize his emotions. His influence on 20th-century Expressionism derives from the psychical significance he attributed to color. "With green and red I have tried to express those terrible things, men's passions."*

The 'Fauve' movement, too, directly stemmed from Van Gogh's art; his handling of color stepped up to its maximum intensity suggested the possibility of using color pure and simple as a constructive element.

1967

G AUGUIN, *too, was to influence 20th-century art both by his discovery of symbolism and by certain aspects of his technique. "To clothe the idea in visual form" was his aim. He thought out his pictures before going to nature. "What beautiful thoughts can be made out of form and colors!"*

He advised his fellow-artists to hark back to the Primitives. Primitives of all descriptions; to their simplified procedures and strong, direct emotions. In his own work, Gauguin applied the method of painting in flat planes, like those of Manet and the Japanese. But he would not hear of imitating nature; for him all art was an abstraction. There was a poetic trend in his make-up which led him to seek out 'equivalences' of forms on the lines of Baudelaire's 'correspondences.' And in Gauguin's art the concept of vision replaced that of observation.

IN THE ART of *Albert Pinkham Ryder, an American contemporary of Van Gogh and Gauguin, we find, as in theirs, a form of symbolism. But his work is highly personal, that of a natural visionary; he was always trying to body forth that which he perceived with his inner eye. The strange enchantments of moonlight, great solitary spaces, the sea at night, or scenes with tragic associations (such as that in which he recalls a friend's suicide) are his favored subjects and he builds them up into compositions all of whose elements are strongly bound together and traversed by vigorous structural rhythms. He selects scenes which symbolize the secret, underlying life of nature and the responses they have aroused in him. But he renders this inner life in a highly simplified manner, he seeks to express only its essential rhythms and thus it is that in his art form is represented in the guise of almost abstract volumes, in which, nevertheless, we feel the presence of a very real, palpitating life.*

Ryder employed his technique solely as a means for giving visible expression to his emotions; that was all he asked of it, and he never gave thought to exploring its full possibilities. He was self-taught, and, at bottom, a primitive. In fact he did not attach any great importance to his means; they were limited but served his purpose. What strikes us most in his temperament is its innocence and purity; and his personality had the strength that these impart—so much so that when he made a trip to Europe he remained,

at the bottom of his artistic self, perfectly impervious to all the influences he encountered and learned nothing from the European artists. Thus it is impossible to associate him with any given school or mode of painting. In short, Ryder was a sort of 'seer' and his deeply moving art lives wholly in the intensity of the colors, which, sufficing in themselves to create the forms, anticipate the discoveries of the 'Fauves.' His art, accorded relatively little attention by his contemporaries, is now appreciated by an ever wider circle and Ryder is seen today as an outstanding figure, indeed one of the most original of American painters.

A. P. RYDER (1847-1917). MOONLIGHT MARINE, 1870-1890. (11 ½ × 11 ¾ ")METRO-POLITAN MUSEUM OF ART, NEW YORK.

TOULOUSE-LAUTREC (1864-1901). THE DANCE OF LA GOULUE, 1895. DETAIL: PORTRAIT OF FÉLIX FÉNÉON. LOUVRE, PARIS.

WITH THIS ADMIRABLE PORTRAIT OF FÉLIX FÉNÉON, THE EMINENT AUTHOR AND CRITIC WHO DID SO MUCH TO PROMOTE THE UNDERSTANDING OF IMPRESSIONISM AND SO ABLY CHAMPIONED THE ART OF THE YOUNGER MEN WHO WERE COMING TO THE FORE AT THE TURN OF THE CENTURY, WE BRING TO A CLOSE OUR PANORAMIC VIEW OF XIXTH-CENTURY PAINTING. IN THE BOLDLY INVENTIVE ART OF TOULOUSE-LAUTREC, WE HAVE A FINE FUSION OF REVOLUTIONARY ELEMENTS AND THOSE CONFORMING TO TRADITION.

BIOGRAPHIES

BIOGRAPHICAL AND BIBLIOGRAPHICAL NOTICES

BONINGTON, RICHARD PARKES

Arnold (Nottingham) 1801 - London 1828.

Born at Arnold, near Nottingham, on October 25, 1801. His father was governor of the Nottingham county jail and a portrait-painter. His family moved to Calais in 1817. There the young man was taught the art of making water-colors in the English fashion by the painter Louis Francia. Then he left for Paris. He entered Baron Gros' studio in 1820 where he formed a friendship with Delacroix, who had the keenest admiration for Bonington's work. During the subsequent years, Bonington often painted in Normandy and Picardy and made frequent visits to London. In 1822, he traveled to Venice. Afterwards, he settled in Hampstead. Exhibited for the first time at the Royal Academy in 1828. Died in London on September 23 of the same year.

Bibl.: BOUVENNE, A. *Catalogue de l'œuvre gravé et litho-graphié*. 1873. — STOKES, Hugh. *Girtin and Bonington*. 1922. DUBUISSON. *R. P. Bonington, his Life and Work*. 1924.

BOUDIN, EUGÈNE

Honfleur 1824 - Deauville 1898.

Born at Honfleur on July 13, 1824, son of an ex-nava gunner. After working in a printing-house at Le Havre he owned a stationery shop and exhibited in his windows pictures by painters who were staying in the district. Encouraged by Millet, he began to paint from nature in 1845. Two canvases he exhibited at Le Havre won him a scholarship from the City Council (1850), which enabled him to study in Paris for three years. On his return to Le Havre he led a hard life which a subsequent stay in Paris did nothing to ameliorate. In 1862, he was at Honfleur in company with Monet and Jongkind. Henceforth, he spent his winters in Paris and his summers in Trouville, Honfleur and Brittany. About 1870, Boudin also painted in Belgium and Holland; gradually he began to be successful. From 1892 onwards, he was forced to spend the winter in Provence because of rheumatism; in 1895, he went as far as Venice. Died at Deauville on August 8, 1898.

Bibl.: G. COHEN. Paris 1900. — L. CARIO. Paris 1929. J. AUBRY. Paris 1922.

CÉZANNE, PAUL

Aix-en-Provence 1839-1906.

Born at Aix-en-Provence (Bouches-du-Rhône) on January 10, 1839. His father was a hat-maker but later took over a bank which had failed, with his associate Cabassol, and made a successful business of it. In 1852 he went to the Collège Bourbon where he met Zola. After taking his baccalauréat, 1859, encouraged by his friends Zola, Coste, Empéraire, Loubon and Valabrègue, he decided to become an artist. In 1861 he went to Paris and attended the Académie Suisse, where he met Pissarro and Guillaumin. He failed at the Ecole des Beaux-Arts. However, he painted some murals for Le Jas de Bouffan, a property which his father had bought near Aix. Returning to Paris in 1864, he met Bazille, Monet, Sisley and Renoir. His works were so wildly romantic that they were regularly rejected by the Salon. In 1866 he protested on this score to the Director of the Beaux-Arts. He now met Manet. Between 1867 and 1870, he traveled in Provence and Paris, and ended up by settling at L'Estaque near Marseilles. In 1873, he moved to Auvers-sur-Oise. He took part in the first Impressionist Exhibition (1874). His contributions to the Salon continued to be rejected. He had to wait until 1882 before he was finally accepted for the first time. In 1866 he married Hortense Fiquet, quarrelled with Zola; his father died, leaving him a large fortune. In 1892 he spent some time at Fontainebleau. This was the period of the various scenes of 'card-players,' 'women bathing' and 'Mont Sainte-Victoire.' He made the acquaintance of Rodin, Clemenceau, Gustave Geffroy (1894). Exhibited at Vollard's for the first time (1895). Settled finally at Aix and exhibited with the Independents (1895). Maurice Denis painted his famous *Homage to Cézanne* (1901). In 1902, he was refused the Legion of Honor which Mirbeau had sought to obtain for him. In 1904, a whole room was devoted to his work at the Salon d'Automne; this was a great success. On October 15, 1906, he had a stroke, and died at Aix on the 22nd of the same month.

Bibl.: VENTURI, L. Paris 1936. — VOLLARD, A. Paris 1914. BERNARD, E. Paris 1921. — MEIER-GRAEFE, J. Munich 1910. — RIVIÈRE, J. Paris 1910. — FAURE, E. Paris 1910. KLINGSOR, T. Paris 1923. — SALMON, A. Paris 1923. FRY, R. New York, London 1927. — ORS, E. d'. Paris 1930. — MACK, G. New York, London 1935. — RAYNAL. M. Paris 1936. — REWALD, J. Paris 1936. — HUYGHE, R. Paris 1936. — NOVOTNY, F. Vienna 1938. — BARNES, A. C. and MAZIA, V. de. New York 1939. — JEDLICKA, G. Zurich 1939. — RILKE, R. M. Paris 1944. — JEWELL, E. A. New York 1944. — LORAN, E. Los Angeles 1946. DORIVAL, B. Paris 1948. — LHOTE, A. Lausanne 1949.

CONSTABLE, JOHN

East Bergholt (Suffolk) 1776 - Hampstead 1837.

Born June 11, 1776, at East Bergholt in Suffolk, where his father was a mill-owner. When he was 19, he showed his first attempts at landscape painting to Joseph Farington, the artist, who gave him advice. He painted in the district in which Gainsborough—whose work he admired so much—had lived. He worked as an amateur until February 1799, when he decided to devote himself entirely to painting and followed the courses at the Royal Academy. While there, he copied many works by Claude Lorrain, Wilson and other landscape-painters. Although he had exhibited his works from 1802 onwards, it was only towards 1811 that his true personality began to make itself felt. His *Hay Wain* was bought by a French collector and shown at the Paris Salon of 1824, where it aroused great interest. His wife died in 1828; this loss depressed him greatly. He was made a member of the Royal Academy in 1829. He died on March 31, 1837.

Bibl.: LESLIE, C. R. *Memoirs of the Life of Constable*. 1845 (standard work). — HOLMES, C. J. *Constable and his Influence on Landscape Painting*. 1902. — CHAMBERLAIN, A. B. *John Constable*. 1903. — WINDSOR, Lord. *John Constable*. 1903.— LINTON, J. D. *Constable's Sketches in Oil and Water-colour*. 1905. — LUCAS, E. V. *Constable the Painter*. 1924.

COROT, CAMILLE

Paris 1796-1875.

His father was a linen-draper from Burgundy; his mother, *née* Oberson, a native of Fribourg (Switzerland), kept a well-known fashion shop in the rue du Bac. After unsuccessfully working as an employee (1817), he obtained his parents' permission to devote himself to painting (1822). He took lessons from Michallon and Bertin, then worked in Paris and the suburbs, in Normandy and the forest of Fontainebleau. From 1825 to 1828, he stayed in Italy, mostly in Rome and the surrounding districts. His family could not induce him to marry and he remained a bachelor all his life. He spent the spring and summer of 1834 in the north of Italy and in 1836 he worked in Provence. In 1837 he gave a *St Jerome* to the church of the town of Avray. The Duke of Orléans bought two of his canvases in 1839. Stayed in French Switzerland (1842), returned there frequently afterwards. Third stay in Italy, in the neighborhood of Rome (1843). Thenceforth worked in every province in France. By approximately 1855, his reputation was made; he produced paintings from life which were little to the public's taste. The Emperor bought the *Souvenir de Marcoussis* for his personal collection. At the World's Fair he was awarded first medal. In 1858, at an auction-sale of his works, 28 canvases fetched 14,230 francs. In 1861, he made another long stay in Fontainebleau. He painted several pictures in London in 1862. In 1866 his *Solitude* was bought by the Emperor who presented it to the Empress. Became a member of the Selection Committee of the Salon in 1870. But in 1874 he was refused the medal of honor which was awarded instead to Gérome. Died on February 22, 1875.

Bibl.: ROBAUT, A. Paris 1905. — MOREAU-NÉLATON, Paris 1924. — FAURE, Elie. Paris 1931. — MEIER-GRAEFE. J. Berlin 1930. — FOSCA, F. Paris 1930. — BAZIN, G., Paris 1942.

COURBET, GUSTAVE

Ornans (Doubs) 1819 - La Tour-de-Peilz (Switzerland) 1877.

His family were vinegrowers in the Franche-Comté. He was an unsatisfactory pupil at the Petit Seminaire in Ornans. His father wished him to enter the Ecole Polytechnique, but finished by letting him go to Paris to study law. What the young Courbet actually did was to rent a studio in the rue de la Harpe (1842) and paint. He visited the Louvre, frequented the 'Académie Suisse,' and painted in the Forest of Fontainebleau. In 1844, one of his canvases was accepted by the Salon. In 1849, his *After Dinner at Ornans* won a second-class medal at the Salon. He became friendly with Champfleury, Prudhon, Baudelaire, Murger. In 1850, he exhibited *The Stone-breakers* and *Funeral at Ornans* at the Salon. He had eleven canvases at the World's Fair Exhibition of 1865. He traveled in Germany (1858-1859). Success at the 1860 Salon; his influence was felt in France, Belgium and Germany. In 1862 he stayed in the Saintonge where he painted in the company of Corot. Manet and Whistler became his pupils in 1865. He refused the Legion of Honor. During the Commune of 1871, he took part in the dismantling of the Vendôme Column. Arrested, he was condemned to six months in prison. In 1873, when the Vendôme proceedings were re-opened, he took refuge in Switzerland and settled down at La Tour-de-Peilz on the Lake of Geneva, His possessions were confiscated and sold. His health grew worse. He died in 1877. His ashes were not transferred to his native village until 1919.

Bibl.: RIAT, G. Paris 1906. — LEMONNIER, Camille. Paris 1878. — GROS-KOST. Paris 1880. — LAZARE, B. Paris 1911. DURET, Th. Paris 1918. — MEIER-GRAEFE, J. Munich 1921. — FONTAINAS, A. Paris 1921. — CHIRICO, G. de. Rome 1925. — LÉGER, Ch. Paris 1929. — COURTHION, P. Paris 1931. — Id. Geneva 1948. — NAEF, H. Bern 1947.

DAUMIER, HONORÉ

Marseilles 1808 - Valmondois 1879.

Born at Marseilles on February 26, 1808. Son of a southern French glass-maker, with a passion for literature. At the age of seven he went to Paris with his parents. At first junior clerk in a process-server's office, then in a book-store, he spent his days at the Louvre. In 1830, he made his first appearance as a caricaturist. He joined the staff of the satirical paper *La Caricature* (1832), and later went over to *Charivari*. His lithographs sometimes had politics for their themes, sometimes manners and morals. He was condemned to six months in prison for his *Gargantua*. Daumier had been painting for a long time without any recognition; it was not until 1848 that he exhibited the sketch for a *Republic*, a subject set for a government competition. But

Daumier did not give up caricature, which was his bread and butter. For this reason he only painted in his rare leisure moments. Apart from his scenes from everyday life and the law courts, he enjoyed depicting print-collectors. He also found many subjects in the plays of Molière and in *Don Quixote*. It was not possible to estimate the importance of his paintings and drawings until the eve of his death. There was an exibition of his works at Durand-Ruel's gallery in 1878. From 1872 onwards, he was threatened with complete blindness and his financial situation was very precarious. His friend Corot generously bought the house in which Daumier was a lodger at Valmondois and made a present of it to him. Daumier died on February 10, 1879.

Bibl.: DURANTY. Paris 1879. — MONTROSIER, E. *La Caricature politique, Honoré Daumier*. Paris 1878. — MARCEL, H. Paris 1906. — KLOSSOWSKI, E. Munich 1908. ROSENTHAL, L. Paris 1912. — HAUSENSTEIN, W. Munich 1918. — WALDEMANN, E. Berlin 1919. — ESCHOLIER, R. Paris 1923. — FONTAINAS, A. Paris 1923. — REY, R. Paris 1923. — BAUDELAIRE, C. *Les dessins de Daumier*. Paris 1924. — SADLER, M. *Daumier, the Man and the Artist*. London 1924. — RUMANN, A. Berlin 1926. — ALEXANDRE, A. Paris 1928. — FOCILLON, H. *Le maître de l'estampe*. Paris 1930. — GRASS-MICK, A. *La Lumière sur Daumier*. Marseille 1931. — FOSCA, F. Paris 1933. — MARX, C. R. Paris 1938. — LASSAIGNE, J. Paris 1938.

DAVID, JACQUES-LOUIS

Paris 1748 - Brussels 1825.

Born in Paris on August 30, 1748, of a family which had owned a haberdashery on the Quai de la Ferraille since the 17th century. From childhood, he showed a passion for drawing. He joined Vien's studio in 1766 and competed several times for the Prix de Rome, although he did not win the first prize until 1774. In 1775 he went to Rome, where he did many drawings from the antique; he stayed there till 1780. The pictures he exhibited at the Salon of 1781 had some measure of success. He was nominated member of the Royal Academy of Painting and Sculpture (1784). Returned to Rome in 1787, so as to paint his *Oath of the Horatii* on the spot; he exhibited it at the 1788 Salon and, like his *The Death of Socrates* of 1787, it caused a great sensation. When the Revolution came, he was an ardent convert to the new ideas and extremist in his views ('78'). Appointed to the Convention, he took part in closing down the Academy, voted for the King's death and became the organizer of all the big, Republican festivals. He was a passionate admirer of Robespierre, after whose downfall he spent six months in prison. Once liberated, he was re-imprisoned, but was ultimately granted an amnesty.

His picture of *The Sabine Women* (1799) won him considerable success. Although a violent Republican, he became a great admirer of Bonaparte, whom he painted crossing the Alps. He was made First Painter to the Emperor in 1804, and commissioned to paint *Le Sacre* (1808 Salon) and the *Distribution of the Eagles* (1810 Salon). When the Bourbons returned in 1816, he had to go into exile (as being a regicide) and sought asylum in Brussels. He died there on September 29, 1825.

Bibl.: GAMOND, T. de. *Vie de David*. Paris 1826. — COUPIN. P. A. *Essai sur J. L. David*. Paris 1827. — LENOIR, A, *David, souvenirs historiques*. Paris 1835. — DELÉCLUSE, E. J. *David, son Ecole et son Temps*. Paris 1815. — SAUNIER, Ch. Paris 1903. — ROSENTHAL, L. Paris, n. d. — DELABORDE, H. *David et l'Ecole française*. Paris 1855. — VAILLAT, L. *David et ses élèves*. Paris 1913. — DAVID, J. *Le peintre Louis David*. Paris 1880. — CANTINELLI, R. Paris 1930. ESCHOLIER, R. *De David à Géricault*. Paris 1941. — VILLARS, Miette de. *Mémoires de David*. Paris 1855. — VALENTINER, U. R. *David and the French Revolution*. New York 1929.

DEGAS, EDGAR

Paris 1834-1917.

Born in Paris on July 19, 1834; his father was a banker, his mother the daughter of a creole lady from New Orleans. As soon as he left the Lycée he showed his natural bent for painting. In 1855, he joined the Ecole des Beaux-Arts, where he met Fantin-Latour and Bonnat. He traveled in Italy (1856-1860). Back in Paris, he turned to the painting of historical subjects. He made the acquaintance of Duranty and Manet. In 1864, he concentrated on portraiture. During the 1870 war he served in the artillery. He met Durand-Ruel, the dealer, in 1872. E. de Goncourt visited him in 1874, the year of the first Impressionist Exhibition, in which he took part. He traveled in Spain in 1880. At the 1881 Salon, exhibited his first sculpture, a dancing-girl in wax. 1885 was the year of his meeting with Gauguin whose work he was one of the first to appreciate. His sight, already impaired, grew progressively worse. He painted dancing-girls and nudes, following a new technique of his own invention in which he mixed oil-paints with pastels. In 1893 he exhibited a series of pastel-landscapes at Durand-Ruel's gallery. He made a collection of paintings, including 20 by Ingres, 13 by Delacroix. About 1900, he became practically blind. His death in Paris on September 27, 1917, during the Great War, passed unnoticed.

Bibl.: *Lettres*. Paris 1931 (new ed. 1945). — LAFOND. Paris 1918-1919. — HERTZ, H. Paris 1920. — MEIER-GRAEFE, J. Munich 1930. — JAMOT, P. Paris 1924. — MANSON, J. B. London 1927. — VALÉRY, Paul. Paris 1938. ROUART, D. Paris 1945. — LEYMARIE, J. Paris 1938. LASSAIGNE, J. Paris 1948. — HAUSENSTEIN, W. Bern 1948. LEMOISNE, P. A. Paris 1946. — REWALD, J. New York 1944.

DELACROIX, EUGÈNE

Charenton 1798 - Paris 1863.

Born April 26, 1798, at Charenton near Paris, he showed as a child a pronounced taste for drawing and music. At the age of sixteen, he became an orphan. After distinguishing himself as a classical scholar, he joined the Ecole des Beaux-Arts, working in Guérin's studio. During this period he copied many works in the Louvre and painted watercolors in the English style with his friends J. B. Soulier and Bonington. His *Dante and Virgil*, exhibited at the 1822 Salon, excited lively criticism, as did his rendering of the *Massacres at Scio* (1824 Salon), which marked him out as one of David's main opponents and a leader of the younger school. During the subsequent years, he painted pictures after subjects taken from history and poetry; he also used the wild beasts in the Jardin des Plantes as models. At the Salon of 1831 he showed, among other works, *Liberty Guiding the People*, his only important canvas on a contemporary national subject. In 1832 he was invited by the Comte de Marnay to accompany him on his mission to the Sultan of Morocco. The journey only lasted six months but it made an indelible impression on the artist. The noble postures of the Arabs draped in their burnouses were, to him, a revelation of the real, as opposed to imaginary, Antiquity. He received his first commission for a mural in 1833: the decoration of the Salon du Roi in the Chambre des Députés. Following this he decorated, in 1838, the library of the Luxembourg Palace; in 1849, the Salon de la Paix at the Hôtel de Ville (burnt down during the Commune) and the Chapel of the 'Saints Anges' in Saint-Sulpice. The 1855 Salon, at which he showed 36 works, was a triumph for him. He was nominated member of the Académie des Beaux-Arts in 1857. Discouraged by the attacks which his contributions to the Salon persistently elicited, he did not exhibit again after 1859. He died in Paris on August 13, 1863.

Bibl.: PIRON. *Delacroix, Sa vie et ses œuvres*. Paris 1865. MOREAU, A. D. Paris 1873. — ROBAUT, E. and CHESNEAU, E.

NÉLATON, E. *Delacroix raconté par lui-même*. Paris 1916. MEIER-GRAEFE, J. Munich 1922. — REGAMEY, E. Paris 1928. — GYSIN, F. Strasbourg 1929. — SIGNAC, P. *D'Eugène Delacroix aux Néo-Impressionnistes*. Paris 1899. MIRBEAU, O. *Des Artistes*. Paris 1922. — ESCHOLIER, R. Paris 1926. — COURTHION, P. *La vie de Delacroix*. Paris 1928. — HOURTICQ, L. Paris 1930. — VENTURI, L. *L'Arte*. 1931. — CASSOU, J. *La gloire de Delacroix*. Paris 1947. FLORISOONE, M. Paris 1947. — DELACROIX. *Journal*. Paris 1926. — DELACROIX. *Lettres*. Paris 1880. — DELACROIX. *Journal*. Translated by Walter Pach. New York 1937. LASSAIGNE, J. Paris 1950.

GAUGUIN, PAUL

Paris 1848 - La Dominique (Marquesas Islands) 1903.

Born in Paris on June 7, 1848. His father was a journalist. After a short voyage to Peru, during which the artist's father died, the Gauguin family returned to Paris. In 1865, Gauguin entered the merchant marine. In 1871 he became a member of the stockbroking firm of Bertin. He married and was in comfortable circumstances. He painted as an amateur and made a collection of works by Manet, Cézanne, Pissarro, Monet and Sisley. He was accepted at the 1876 Salon. After the Stock-Exchange slump of 1883, he left the financial world and devoted himself exclusively to painting. In 1885, he quarreled with his family; a period of extreme poverty ensued. He became a bill-poster. First stay at Pont-Aven in 1886. Meeting with Emile Bernard and Van Gogh. Journey to Martinique in 1887. At Arles, in 1888, quarreled with Van Gogh, who cut off his own ear. At the World's Fair of 1889, Gauguin was greatly struck by Japanese art. He exhibited some of his work at the Café Volpini. The public was highly amused but the young painters Sérusier, Denis and Bonnard were much impressed. At this period Gauguin was without a home and lived with his friend Schuffenecker. In 1891, he decided to leave for Tahiti where he did much work, but he had to return to Paris for lack of money. He stayed in France for two years, then, in 1895, decided to return to Oceania. This time he remained there until his death on May 8, 1903, at Dominica, in the Marquesas.

Bibl.: *Lettres*. Paris 1919, 1920, 1946; New York 1943 (edited by J. Rewald). — ROTONCHAMP, J. de. Paris 1906. MORICE, C. Paris 1919. — CHASSÉ. C. Paris 1921. — DORSENNE, J. Paris 1927. — BARTH, W. Basel 1929. MAUGHAM, W. S. London and New York. — ALEXANDRE, A. Paris 1930. — COGNIAT, R. Paris 1936. — GAUGUIN, Pola. Paris 1938. — REWALD, J. Paris and London 1938. BERNARD E. Lorient 1941. — WITT, A. de. Milan 1946. MALINGUE. Paris 1948. — TARALON, J. Paris 1949.

GÉRICAULT, THÉODORE

Rouen 1791-1824.

Born at Rouen on September 26, 1791, of a middle-class family. Coming to Paris with his family while still young, he soon showed that his consuming passions were horses and painting. He became a pupil in Carle Vernet's studio in 1805 and two years later joined Guérin's atelier where he met Delacroix in 1817. Meanwhile he did much copying at the Louvre. He achieved great success when he exhibited his *Officier de Chasseurs de la Garde Impériale* at the 1812 Salon. On the other hand, the *Wounded Cuirassier* met with a poor reception at the Salon of 1814. During the Hundred Days, he enlisted in the Musketeers and followed King Louis XVIII to Béthune. He left for Italy, visited Florence and Rome in 1816. His *Raft of the Medusa*, shown at the Salon of 1819, gave rise to a scandal. He stayed in England in 1820 where the latter picture was shown in various towns. On his return to France, he was the victim of a riding-accident which kept him in bed for many months.

He seemed to have recovered by the end of 1822, but there was a relapse and he died on January 26, 1824.

Bibl.: CLEMENT, Ch. Paris 1879. — REGAMEY, R. Paris 1926. OPRESCO, G. Paris 1927. — PILON, E. *Constance Mayer.* Paris 1927. — ESCHOLIER, R. *De David à Géricault.* Paris 1941. — BERGER, Klaus. *Gericault's Drawings and Water-colours.* London 1946. — MARTINE, Ch. *Dessins de Géricault.* Paris 1929.

GOYA Y LUCIENTES, FRANCISCO DE

Fuendetodos (Aragon) 1746 - Bordeaux 1828.

Born on March 30, 1746, in the village of Fuendetodos in Aragon. His father was first a gilder, then a cultivator. Took his first lessons from a painter named Lujan, and attended drawing-classes at Saragossa. In 1763 he went to Madrid, and in 1771 made the traditional 'journey to Italy,' where he won a prize in a competition organized by the Parma Academy. Returning to Spain, he painted murals in the church of S. Maria del Pilar at Saragossa and in a near-by Carthusian convent. At Madrid (1776) got his first commission for tapestry cartoons; next year fell seriously ill. In 1780 was made a member of the Royal Academy of San Fernando. While doing more work for churches, he won much renown with his portraits of men and women of high society. Appointed court painter in 1789. After a nervous breakdown in 1793, he became almost totally deaf; this, however, is the period when the almost fifty-year-old painter is said to have had a love affair with the proud and capricious Duchess of Alba. In 1798, decorated the dome of San Antonio de la Florida. (near Madrid), and next year completed his first series of etchings, the 'Caprichos.' In 1800, painted the big group portrait of the Spanish Royal Family, and some time before 1802, his two famous pictures, *La Maja Vestida* and *La Maja Desnuda.* During the French occupation (1808) he showed no open hostility to the invaders, as he consented to paint King Joseph's portrait and to sit on the committee appointed to select the pictures to be delivered to Napoleon. But at the time of the 1812 uprising, he painted two large canvases depicting the revolt of the people of Madrid and the brutal reprisals that ensued. He also executed a series of engravings *The Disasters of War,* published in 1863. The *Bull-Fights* series was made in 1815; the *Proverbs* series published in 1864. On the return of Ferdinand VII, Goya was not molested in any way ; indeed the king commissioned him to paint his portrait. In 1819 Goya bought a simple country-house known as 'The Deaf Man's House' near Madrid and covered the walls with paintings. In 1824 he obtained leave of absence to visit sulphur-springs in France (because of his gout), but actually he settled down at Bordeaux, where he took to lithography. He made a brief trip to Madrid two years later. Died at Bordeaux, April 16, 1828.

Bibl.: CALVERT, A. F. London 1908. — LOGA, L. von. Berlin 1903. — LAFOND, P. Paris 1913. — BERUETE, Aureliano de. Madrid 1915. — MATHERON, J. Paris 1858. YRIARTE, Ch. Paris 1867. — LEFORT, P. Paris 1877. — SANCHEZ, Zaferino Araujo. Madrid 1895. — ROTHENSTEIN, W. London 1900. — MUTHER, R. Berlin 1906. — BERTELES, Kurt. Munich 1907. — MAYER, A. L. Munich 1923. D'ORS, E. 1928. — CANTON, Sanchez. Paris 1929. — VALLENTIN, A. Paris 1951. — LASSAIGNE, J. Paris 1949. POORE, Charles. New York 1939. — MAYER, August L. London 1929.

INGRES, JEAN-DOMINIQUE

Montauban 1780 - Paris 1867.

Ingres was born at Montauban on the 29th August 1780. His father devoted himself to sculpture and painting. After working at Toulouse, he reached Paris at the age of 17 and entered David's studio (1797). Until 1806, he lived in Paris where he painted portraits. Then he went to Italy. He lived in Rome for 18 years and afterwards in Florence, painting alternately portraits and mythological subjects. (He remained there until 1824.) He married a young milliner, Madeleine Chapelle, who joined him in Italy (1813). The works he sent to the Salons of 1814 and 1819 were not appreciated. However, he received a State commission, the *Vœu de Louis XIII* and this canvas, exhibited at the 1824 Salon, brought him such great success that he decided to settle in Paris. Orders flowed in and he opened a studio which immediately became very popular. In 1834 he exhibited his *Martyrdom of Saint Symphorien* but it was bitterly criticized. Deeply hurt, Ingres sought and obtained the post of director of the French Academy at Rome. He arrived in Rome at the end of the year and stayed there until 1841. Ingres exhibited *Stratonice* in Paris (1840). This was a real triumph and he emerged as the undeniable leader of the classical school. The painter then returned to Paris. At the request of the Duke de Luynes (1843), he agreed to paint two large decorative works, *The Golden Age* and *The Iron Age* in the Château de Dampierre. But, in 1848, the artist abandoned the task and left *The Iron Age* unfinished. His wife died in 1851. The next year he married Mlle Delphine Ramel, who was a great deal younger than he. In the years that followed, honors were showered on him. He died on January 8, 1867 from the after-effects of a cold.

Bibl.: LAPAUZE, H. Paris 1911. — FRÖHLICH-BUM. Vienna 1924. — JAMOT, P. *Revue de l'Art ancien et moderne.* Paris 1920. — MOMMEJA. *Gazette des Beaux-Arts.* 1926. JAMOT, P. *Musées de France.* Paris 1911. — PACH, Walter. New York 1939. — GAUTIER, Th. *Les Beaux-arts en Europe.* Paris 1855. — BLANC, Ch. *Ingres, sa vie et ses œuvres.* Paris 1870. — AMAURY-DUVAL. *L'atelier d'Ingres.* Paris 1878. — BALZE, R. *Ingres par un de ses élèves.* Paris 1880. — MONROND. Paris 1869. — MERSON, O. Paris 1870. MONTROZIER. 1882. — DEBIA. *Souvenirs intimes.* Montauban 1868. — HOURTICQ, L. Paris 1928. — ALAZARD, J. *Ingres et l'ingrisme.* Paris 1949. — HOMMEJA. *La correspondance d'Ingres.* Paris 1888. — LAPAUZE. *Extraits des cahiers manuscrits de l'artiste.* Cosmopolis 1898. — INGRES. *Pensées.* La Sirène, Paris.

JONGKIND, JOHANN-BARTHOLD

Latrop (Holland) 1819 - Grenoble 1891.

Born June 3, 1819, in a hamlet in the province of Over-Yssel in Holland, and was the eighth child of a clergyman. At first studied under Shelhout, a landscapist, at the Academy of the Hague and obtained a Royal Stipend. In 1845 made the acquaintance of the French landscape-painter Isabey and a year later left for Paris. Worked in the Seine estuary and on the Normandy sea-coast; from 1848 to 1860 divided his time between Holland and Paris. He led a life of alcoholism and debauchery which turned his best friends away from him and resulted in his grant being withdrawn. Overwhelmed by debts, he was on the verge of madness. Finally a small Parisian picture-dealer, Martin, generously came to his rescue and Madame Fesser, a Dutch painter married to a chef, devoted herself entirely to him. From now on painted watercolors during the summer in Normandy (in 1862 at Le Havre with Monet and Boudin), Belgium and Holland; during the winter worked in his studio. Exhibited 3 canvases at the Salon des Refusés in 1863. His work which had deteriorated greatly during the period of his heavy drinking began to show an improvement. His paintings were in great demand by art-dealers and connoisseurs. From 1873 onwards he painted mostly in Dauphiné, where he lived with Madame Fesser. But during his later years he was subject to attacks of raving insanity and suffered from persecution mania. He died on February 9, 1891, in an insane asylum at Grenoble.

Bibl.: MOREAU-NÉLATON, E. Paris 1918. — COLIN, P. Paris 1921. — SIGNAC, P. Paris 1927.

MANET, Edouard

Paris 1832-1883.

Born in Paris on January 25, 1832. His father, then magistrate, rose to be a judge of appeal. Manet studied at the Collège Rollin (1842), where he was a boarder. His parents were not in favor of his taking up art as a career. He decided to join the navy but failed the entrance examination for the Naval School. His parents yielded eventually and Manet entered Couture's studio (1850 to 1856). He traveled in Holland, Germany, Austria and Italy, visiting the museums. In 1859 *The Absinthe Drinker* was rejected at the Salon in spite of Delacroix' commendation. He met Baudelaire and at the 1861 Salon showed his painting, the *Guitarrero*, which won him a medal. In 1863 exhibited *Le Déjeuner sur l'herbe* at the Salon des Refusés. The picture created a scandal but the younger artistic set were enthusiastic about it. *Olympia* (1865) had an equally hostile reception at the Salon. Manet met Cézanne, Mallarmé, Monet and Zola, who was championing the 'new' painting in the newspaper *L'Evénement*. Manet served as a lieutenant in the National Guard during the war of 1870. He began to be successful from 1872 onwards, the public having become favorably disposed towards him. Despite pressure by Degas and Monet, he refused to take part in the First Impressionist Exhibition (1874). *Le Linge* was rejected by the Salon of 1876 and *Nana* by the 1877 Salon. In 1879, illness forced him to submit to treatment. By 1880 his studio had become a meeting-place for artists and society people. He was made Chevalier of the Legion of Honor in 1881. In 1883 his health grew much worse. He was confined to his room, where he made paintings of flowers. His left leg was amputated on April 18, and he died on April 30, 1883.

Lettres. Paris 1929. — DURET, T. Paris 1902. — TABARANT, A. Paris 1931. — ZOLA, E. Paris 1867. — BAZIRE, E. Paris 1884. — WALDMANN, E. Berlin 1910. — PROUST, A. Paris 1913. — BLANCHE, J. E. Paris 1924. — MOREAU-NELATON. Paris 1926. — REY, R. Paris 1938. — JEDLICKA, G. Zurich 1941. — COURTHION, P. Geneva 1945. — FLORISOONE, M. Monaco 1947.

MILLET, Jean-François

Gruchy (Manche) 1815 - Barbizon 1875.

Born October 4, 1815, at Gruchy near Cherbourg, of peasant stock. Took his first lessons from an old painter living at Cherbourg, and obtained a grant enabling him to go to Paris, where he enrolled in Delaroche's class. In 1840 exhibited at the Salon for the first time (a portrait). Eked out a living by painting canvases for picture-dealers. His *Winnower* in the 1848 Salon attracted much attention. In 1849 removed to Barbizon with his family and devoted himself to rustic subjects exclusively. For many years had a struggle to keep afloat, both critics and connoisseurs disliking his landscapes as being too 'realistic.' The tide turned in 1853. *The Angelus* is dated 1859. During the 1870 war he moved to Cherbourg, where he painted seascapes. The Government gave him a commission for a set of panels for the Panthéon; he made the sketches but was never able to execute the paintings. Died January 20, 1875.

Bibl.: CLARETIE, J. Paris 1882. — FREMINE, C. *Au pays de Millet*. Paris. — LAURIN, C. J. Stockholm 1907. — MARX, Roger. Paris 1897. — MOREAU-NELATON, E. *Millet raconté par lui-même*. Paris 1921. — SENSIER, A. *La vie et l'œuvre de Millet*. Paris 1881. — YRIARTE, C. Paris 1885. — SOULIER, L. Paris 1900. — ENSEL, W. *Millet und Rousseau*. Leipzig 1912. — CARTWRIGHT, J. *J. F. Millet, his Life and Letters*. London 1896. — CAIN and LEPRIEUR. Paris 1913. — JACQUES, F. *Le livre d'or de Millet*. Paris. MARCEL, H. Paris. — MUTHER, R. Berlin. — PIEDAGNEL, A. *Millet, souvenirs de Barbizon*. Paris 1876. — STALEY. London 1905. — THOMSON, A. *J. F. Millet and the Barbizon School*. London 1908.

MONET, Claude

Paris 1840 - Giverny (Eure) 1926.

Born in Paris on February 14, 1840. His parents were grocers. He spent his childhood and youth at Le Havre where he met Boudin, who introduced him to landscape painting when he was only 18 years old. In 1859 he went to Paris, met Troyon, copied pictures at the Louvre and attended the Académie Suisse where he became friendly with Pissarro. He returned to Le Havre in 1862, after his military service, in company with Boudin and Jongkind. In Paris, he met Renoir and Sisley in Gleyre's studio. 1863 was the year of his rendez-vous with Renoir, Bazille and Sisley at Barbizon. A seascape was accepted at the Salon in the following year. In 1865, he joined Courbet at Trouville. Life was extremely hard for him. Two hundred of his pictures were seized and sold in lots at 30 to 50 francs a lot. He went to London in 1870 and met Pissarro there. Daubigny introduced him to Durand-Ruel, the art dealer. From 1872 to 1878, Monet settled at Argenteuil. His studio was a house-boat. Accepted as the leader of the Impressionists, he influenced Renoir, Sisley, Manet. At the first group exhibition (1874), he showed a picture called *Impression: Sunrise* which was the origin of the term 'Impressionism'. In 1878 Monet was at Vétheuil. He lost his wife Camille, his financial difficulties increased. It was not until 1883 that a small measure of success allowed him to settle at Giverny. Nevertheless, he traveled a great deal: Bordighera, Antibes, London, where he got to know Turner's work, Norway, Venice, etc. His sight deteriorated but he was successfully operated on for cataract (1922). He gave his *Waterlilies* to the Nation and they were installed at the Orangerie in the Tuileries gardens. He spent the last years of his life as a recluse at Giverny where he was often visited by his friend Clemenceau. He died on December 6, 1926.

Bibl.: MIRBEAU, O. 1891. — ALEXANDRE, A. Paris 1921. GEFFROY, G. Paris 1922. — WERTH, L. Paris 1928. CLEMENCEAU, G. Paris 1928. — FELS, M. DE. Paris 1929. FRANCASTEL, P. Paris 1939. — MALINGUE, M. Monaco 1943.

PISSARRO, Camille

Saint-Thomas (West Indies) 1830 - Paris 1903.

Born at Saint-Thomas in the West Indies, July 10, 1830, of Jewish parents. After studying in Paris, he returned to Saint-Thomas to work in his father's business. In 1855, his parents agreed to his becoming an artist and sent him to Paris. After a short period at the Ecole des Beaux-Arts, he attended the Académie Suisse, exhibited at the 1859 Salon, met Monet and later, in 1861, Cézanne and Guillaumin. In 1863 he showed three landscapes at the Salon des Refusés. In 1866 went to live in Pontoise, and three years later in Louveciennes. Durand-Ruel bought two of his paintings in 1871. His studio was looted by the Germans—out of 1500 paintings, only some 40 remained. In 1872 he introduced Cézanne to Impressionism and in 1874 took part in the First Impressionist Exhibition. He met Gauguin (1877), Signac and Seurat (1885), Van Gogh (1886). He adopted the Pointillist technique, but later abandoned it. Prosperity came to him in the end and in 1892 he gave a big exhibition at Durand-Ruel's gallery. Died in Paris, November 13, 1903.

Bibl.: LECOMTE, G. Paris 1922. — TABARANT, A. Paris 1924. — KUNSTLER, C. Paris 1930. — REWALD, J. *Burlington Magazine*. 1938. — FRANCASTEL, P. Paris 1939. REWALD, J. Paris 1939.

RENOIR, Pierre-Auguste

Limoges 1841 - Cagnes 1919.

Born at Limoges (Haute-Vienne) on February 25, 1841. His father was a small tailor. In 1845, the Renoir family moved to Paris. Young Auguste attended the grammar school. At the age of 13 he was sent by his parents to a china factory. There he acquired a taste for decoration and color and began to paint designs on vases and later on fans. He paid frequent visits to the Louvre. At the age of 21, he entered the Ecole des Beaux-Arts (Gleyre's studio) where he met Monet, Sisley and Bazille, His first work, at the 1864 Salon, was an *Esmeralda* which he later destroyed. In 1866 he worked in the Forest of Fontainebleau and at Marlotte. His work was not accepted at the Salon in spite of the intervention of Corot and Daubigny. The following year his *Diane Chasseresse* was also refused. Life was difficult for him. Monet and Renoir joined each other at Bougival in 1869; they painted the same subjects, notably several versions of the *Grenouillère*. These were the first productions in the Impressionist style. During the 1870 War, Renoir was in the 10th Light Cavalry. In 1873, Durand-Ruel bought some of his pictures. Renoir took part in the first exhibition by the Impressionist group at Nadar's gallery in 1874. A sale of works by Renoir, Monet and Sisley, etc., held at the Hôtel Drouot was a complete disaster (1875).

Renoir left the Impressionist movement, preferring to exhibit at the Salon (1885). Cézanne welcomed him at Le Jas de Bouffan in 1888.

From 1899, he was forced by rheumatism to seek the climate of the South of France. A retrospective exhibition of his works at the Salon d'Automne in 1904 was a triumph. A stroke deprived him of the use of arms and legs (1912). He worked with a brush tied to his hand. He died at Cagnes on December 3, 1919.

Bibl.: ANDRÉ, A. & ELDER, M. Paris 1931. — MIRBEAU, O. Paris 1913. — VOLLARD, A. Paris 1919 and 1920. — RIVIÈRE, G. Paris 1921. — ANDRÉ, A. Paris 1919 and 1928. ALEXANDRE, A. Paris 1920. — DURET, Th. Paris 1924. BESSON, G. Paris 1929. — BERARD, M. Paris 1938. — MEIER-GRAEFE, J. Munich 1911, Leipzig 1929. — DUTHUIT, G. Paris 1923. — BARNES, A. & MAZIA, V. de. Paris 1944. DRUCKER, M. Paris 1944 (new ed., 1949). — REWALD, J. New York 1946. — RAYNAL, M. Geneva 1949.

ROUSSEAU, THÉODORE

Paris 1812 - Barbizon 1867.

He was born in Paris on April 15, 1812, the son of a tailor who intended him for the Polytechnic. At first he took lessons from the landscape painter, Charles Rémond, and Guillou-Lethière, but developed his talents primarily by working from nature. He was deeply impressed by the Constable landscapes shown at the 1832 Salon. Some of his works in the 18th century style appeared at the Salon from 1831 to 1834 but from 1836 to 1848 his contributions were steadily rejected. He was, however, vigorously supported by the critics, particularly by Thoré-Bürger. It was during this period that he painted the *Descente des Vaches*, *Allée de Châtaigniers*, *Marais dans les landes* and *Effet de givre*. In 1815, he exhibited *Edge of the Forest* and *Clearing in the Forest of Fontainebleau*. He had stayed at Barbizon several times but did not settle there permanently until 1848. His last years were clouded by the illness of his wife, who lost her mind. He died on December 22, 1867.

Bibl.: ENSEL, W. *Millet und Rousseau*. Leipzig 1912. BAZIN, R. *Deux peintres de Barbizon, Millet et Rousseau*. Paris, " Revue hebdomadaire ", 1910. — HUYGHE, R. et JACOTTET, P. *Le dessin français au XIXe siècle*. Paris. MICHEL, Emile. *Les Maîtres du paysage français*. Paris 1906. — SENSIER, A. *Souvenirs sur Rousseau*. Paris 1872.

RYDER, ALBERT PINKHAM

New Bedford (Massachusetts) 1847 - Elmhurst (N.Y.) 1917.

Born in 1847, at New Bedford, Massachusetts, U.S.A., he went with his family to New York in 1867. He learned the rudiments of art from the engraver William E. Marshall, who had studied in Paris. In 1871, he studied at the National Academy and lived in an uncomfortable studio, where he worked for the rest of his life in chaotic conditions and often in penury. He did make one journey to Europe but his style of painting was completely unaffected by foreign influences. He continued to work alone, without method, discovering painting for himself, as it were. He even went so far as to cut panels from his bedstead, when he was short of canvases. He died at Elmhurst, ill and poverty-stricken at the age of 70 in 1917 at the home of one of his students who had taken him in.

Bibl.: PRICE, F. N. *Ryder: A Study in Appreciation*. New York. — SHERMAN, F. F. *A. P. Ryder*. New York.

SEURAT, GEORGES

Paris 1859-1891.

Born in Paris on December 2, 1859, Seurat was the son of a bailiff. When he left high school, he attended the Municipal School of Design and visited museums and libraries. He copied Holbein, Raphael, Poussin and Ingres. In 1878, he entered the Ecole des Beaux-Arts. He studied the scientific treatises of Chevreul and Charles Blanc. From 1881 to 1887, he concentrated exclusively on drawing. Later he painted his first pictures with small, separate touches and glowing shadings; a technique given the name 'Divisionism.' In 1884, his *Baignade* was rejected at the Salon but accepted and exhibited the same year at the first Salon des Indépendants, along with works by Cross, Signac, Redon, etc. In 1885, he met Pissarro who became a disciple of 'Divisionism.' Seurat painted his *Sunday Afternoon on the Island of La Grande Jatte*. He put several months of work into this painting, 38 studies and 23 drawings. The picture roused a storm of protest. Fénéon published a critical analysis of the painting in *La Vogue*. In the same year (1886), it was exhibited in New York. At the 4th Salon des Indépendants (1888) his *Parade* and *Poseuses* were exhibited. In 1891, Seurat was present at the Symbolist banquet given on February 3, presided over by Mallarmé and attended by Barrès, France, Gide, Renard, Gauguin, Mirbeau, Redon, etc. Seurat was working on his major composition, the *Cirque*, when he died of a fever on March 29, 1891. He was only 32 years old.

Bibl.: CHRISTOPHE, J. Paris 1890. — SALMON, A. Brussels 1921. — COUSTURIER, L. Paris 1921. — LHOTE, A. Rome 1922, Paris 1947. — PACH, W. New York 1923. — COQUIOT. Paris 1924. — KAHN, G. Paris 1926. — GEORGE, W. Paris 1928. — ROGER-MARX, C. Paris 1931. — RICH, D.C. Chicago 1935. — REWALD, J. New York 1943, Paris 1947. LAPRADE, J. de. Monaco 1945. — COOPER, D. London 1946. — BERTRAM, H. Copenhagen 1946. — SELIGMAN, New York 1947.

SISLEY, ALFRED

Paris 1839 - Moret 1899.

Born in Paris October 30, 1839; of English stock. After a stay in London where he tried his hand at a business career, he returned to Paris and enrolled in Gleyre's studio (1862). There he met Monet, Renoir, Bazille. From 1865 on, he painted in Fontainebleau Forest. Two of his canvases were accepted for the 1866 Salon. A regular visitor to the Café Guerbois in 1869, taking part in the confabulations that led up to Impressionism. In London in 1871, he entered into contact with Durand-Ruel. Even after his family had been ruined, he went on painting, though under the most trying material conditions. Between 1872 and 1880, he worked exclusively in the neighborhood of Paris, painting at Marly, Louveciennes, Bougival, Meudon and Argenteuil, where he joined forces with Monet. His paintings at the 1875 Hôtel Drouot sale fetched from 50 to 700 francs apiece. In 1883, he retired to live at Les Sablons, near Moret. He never became rich or famous during his life. Died January 29, 1899, of cancer of the throat.

Bibl.: WATSON, F., in *The Arts*. 1921. — GEFFROY, G. Paris 1923. — SISLEY, C., in *Burlington Magazine*. 1949. JEDLICKA, G. Bern 1949.

TOULOUSE-LAUTREC, Henri de

Albi 1864 - Malromé (Tarn) 1901.

Born at Albi in the province of Tarn on November 24, 1864. He was a direct descendant of the Counts of Toulouse, ennobled under Charlemagne. In 1872 he went to Paris and studied at the Lycée Fontanes. He was not robust and two successive accidents, in which he broke both legs, left him deformed. He dedicated himself to painting, encouraged in this by his parents. In 1882, he entered the Ecole des Beaux-Arts (at first in Bonnat's and later in Cormon's studio) but at the same time discovered Manet and Degas. In 1886, after meeting Van Gogh, he settled in Montmartre where the atmosphere gave him inspiration. He became friendly with the dancers Valentin le Désossé, Jane Avril, Grille d'Egout, La Goulue. In 1889 he exhibited at the Salon des Indépendants. He drew posters in the Japanese style, then decorated La Goulue's booth at the Foire du Trône in 1895. He made his home in the Avenue Frochot in 1897, painting nudes, sporting scenes, the circus and numerous portraits. In 1898 he made a trip to London. His health was affected by the irregular life he led and in 1899 he was confined in an asylum at Neuilly. Set free thanks to a press campaign, he traveled a short while but excessive drinking caused his health to deteriorate again. Paralyzed by a stroke, he arranged to be taken to his mother's house at Malromé (Tarn) and died on September 9, 1901, aged 37.

Bibl.: JOYANT, Maurice. Paris 1921. — DELTEIL, L. Paris 1920. — JULIEN, E. Albi 1939. — ESSWEIN, H. Munich 1904. — COQUIOT, G. Paris 1913. — DURET, T. Paris 1920. LAPPARENT, P. de. Paris 1927. — JEDLICKA, G. Berlin 1929. MAC ORLAN, P. Paris 1934. — SCHAUB-KOCH. Paris 1935. TOURETTE, G. de la. Paris 1939. — JULIEN, E. Monaco 1942. — ROTZLER, W. Paris 1946. — DELAROCHE-VERNET HENRAUX, H. Paris 1948. — SCHMIDT, G. Basel 1948.

TURNER, Joseph Mallord William

London 1775-1851.

Son of a London hairdresser and a mother who died insane, Turner was born on April 23, 1775, in London. As a boy he showed a gift for drawing and was given lessons in perspective and architectural design. In 1797 exhibited his first oil painting at the Royal Academy; it attracted much attention. In 1799 elected an Associate of the Royal Academy, and in 1802 an R. A. Painted sea-pieces inspired by Claude Lorrain and Poussin. He was now a successful artist and his pictures fetched very high prices. Peace having been made between England and France, he started (in 1802) a long ramble on the Continent, visiting Burgundy, the Dauphiné, Haute Savoie, the Bernese Oberland, St Gothard and Basel. In 1817 he went to Belgium and traveled down the Rhine from Coblenz to Mainz. In 1819-1820 he roamed Italy, in 1825 Holland, in 1826 the country round the Meuse and the Moselle. In 1830 he visited Venice. In 1841 he returned to Switzerland, and put in long stays in that country in 1843-1844. Gradually he altered his style, his renderings of nature grew more and more grandiose, his technique freer and more original, his color brighter. Public taste did not keep pace with him, but this did not trouble him; with the years he was becoming more and more aloof from others. He took to drinking and began to lead a double life under the name of 'Mr. Rooth.' He died on December 19, 1851, bequeathing to the National Gallery over 300 oil-paintings and many thousands of watercolors and drawings.

Bibl.: RUSKIN. Modern Painters. 1843-1860. — BURNET, CUNNINGHAM and MURRAY. Turner and his Works. 1859. THORNBURY. Life. 1877. — HAMERTON, P. G. Life. 1879. MONKHOUSE. Turner. 1879. — WEDMORE, F. Turner and Ruskin. 1900. — ARMSTRONG, W. Turner. 1902 (with list of works by E. Dillon). — RAWLINSON, W. G. Turner's Liber Studiorum. 1906.

VAN GOGH, Vincent

Groot-Zundert (Holland) 1853 - Auvers-sur-Oise 1890.

Born March 30, 1853, at Groot-Zundert (Holland). His father was a clergyman; his family included clergymen, sailors and patrons of art. In 1869, he was employed at the Goupil art-gallery at the Hague, then in Brussels. He read a great deal and visited museums. He lived for a time in London, then in Paris, returning ultimately to Amsterdam to prepare himself for admission to the theological seminary. After failing the examination he began preaching to the miners in the Borinage but lived in abject poverty. About 1880, he took up painting although opposed by his father in this choice of career. Van Gogh sought the advice of his cousin Mauve, a painter, who helped him considerably. In 1882, he did his first oil painting and in addition produced drawings, watercolors and lithographs. He returned to his father's home in Nuenen and worked furiously. In 1885, he painted his *Potatoe-Eaters*. 1886 was his Antwerp period. Then he decided to leave for Paris. During his Paris period (1886-1888) he met Gauguin, Lautrec, Seurat, Degas, Pissarro and others. His Arles period followed (1888-1889). He discovered the Mediterranean. During a violent quarrel with Gauguin, he cut off his own ear. He was confined at Arles. Two hundred of his pictures date from this period. At his own request, he was treated in the asylum at Saint-Rémy. He had periods of lucidity between spells of madness. In 1890, at the exhibition of 'Les Vingt,' the only painting he ever sold in his life *(The Red Vines)* was bought for 200 francs. In May 1890, he arrived in Auvers-sur-Oise and became the patient and friend of Doctor Gachet. But on July 27, 1890, during one of his crises, he shot himself in the chest with a revolver. He died two days later; his last words were, "There'll never be an end to human misery."

Bibl.: *Lettres.* Paris 1947. — FAILLE, J. B. de la. Paris and Brussels 1928. — BERNARD, E. Amsterdam 1915. MEIER-GRAEFE, J. Munich 1921. — PIERARD, L. Paris 1924. — FRY, R. London 1926. — FLORISOONE, M. Paris 1937. — UHDE, W. Vienna 1936. — BREUCKEN, J. de. Liège 1938, Brussels 1945. — HUYGHE, R. Paris 1938. NIGG, W. Bern 1942. — MUENSTENBERG, W. London and Paris 1947. — SCHMIDT, G. Bern 1947. — HAMMACHER, A. M. Amsterdam 1948. — NORDENFALF, C. Amsterdam 1948. — TRABAULT, M. Amsterdam 1948. — DUTHUIT, G. Lausanne 1949. — BROOKS, C. M. New York 1942 (compl. bibliography).

WHISTLER, James

Lowell (Massachusetts) 1834 - London 1903.

James Abbott McNeill Whistler was born on July 10, 1834, at Lowell (Mass.). In early youth at St Petersburg, where his father had been given an engineering post; then a student at West Point. But he soon decided to make his career in art. Came to Paris when he was twenty-two, made copies at the Louvre, struck up friendships with Fantin-Latour and Manet. In 1862 painted the *White Girl*; rejected by the 1863 official Salon, it was exhibited at the 'Salon des Refusés.' Moved to London that year. Was much influenced by Japanese art and painted *Nocturnes* which had some influence on American art; but his work still met with little favor and Ruskin violently disapproved of it. In 1883 painted the portrait of Théodore Duret. In 1885 lectured in London, Oxford and Cambridge. Returned to Paris in 1892 and enjoyed great success. Was made a Chevalier, then an Officier, of the French Legion of Honor. Traveled to South Africa and Sicily. In 1902 visited Holland; had a heart-attack, but recovered enough to return to London. Died in 1903, aged 69.

Bibl.: *The Gentle Art of making Enemies.* 1890. — MANSFIELD, H. *Descriptive Catalogue of Etchings and Drypoints.* 1905. — LEVY, F. N. *Catalogue of Paintings in Oil and*

Pastel. Metropolitan Museum. New York 1910. — *Catalogue of Works*. Victoria and Albert Museum. London. *Whistleriana*. Freer Gallery. Washington 1928. — BERALDI, H. *Les Graveurs du XIXe siècle*. Vol. 12. 1892. — WEDMORE, F. *Whistler's Etchings*. 1899. — WAY, R. and DENNIS, G. R. *The Art of J. M. Whistler*. 1903. — MENPES. *Whistler as I knew Him*. 1904. — EDDY, A. J. *Recollections and Impressions of Whistler*. 1903. — PENNELL, J. and E. R. *Life*. 1908. — SEITZ, D. C. *Writings by and about Whistler: a Bibliography*. Edinburgh 1910.

GENERAL BIBLIOGRAPHY

CHENEY, Sheldon. *History of Modern Art*. New York 1945.

DIMIER, Louis. *Histoire de la peinture française au XIXe siècle*. Paris 1914.

BLANCHE, J. E. *De David à Degas*. Paris 1919.

FONTAINAS, A. and VAUXCELLES, L. *Histoire générale de l'art français de la Révolution à nos jours*. Paris 1922.

FOCILLON, H. *La peinture au XIXe et au XXe siècle*. Paris 1928.

SCHNEIDER, R. *L'art français au XIXe siècle*. Paris 1929.

ISHAM. *American Painting*. New York 1927.

REAU, L. *L'art français aux Etats-Unis*. Paris 1926.

MEIER-GRAEFE, J. *Entwicklungsgeschichte der modernen Kunst*. Berlin 1915.

SCHEFFLER, K. *Die europäische Kunst im XIX. Jahrhundert*. Berlin 1929.

REAU, L. *Histoire universelle des Arts*. Paris 1936.

SOMARE, E. *Storia dei Pittori italiani dell'ottocento*. Milan 1928.

PAULI, G. *Die Kunst des Klassizismus und der Romantik*. Berlin 1925.

ROSENTHAL, L. *La Peinture romantique*. Paris 1900.

ALAZARD, J. *L'Orient et la peinture française au XIXe siècle*. Paris 1930.

REAU, L. *L'Art romantique*. Paris 1930.

SIZERANNE, R. de la. *La Peinture anglaise contemporaine*. Paris 1895.

HUNT, Holman. *Preraphaelitism and the Preraphaelite Brotherhood*. London 1905.

BATE, Percy H. *The English Pre-Raphaelite Painters*. London 1899.

DORBEC, P. *L'Art du paysage en France*. Paris 1925.

NASSE. *Deutsche Maler der Frühromantik*. Munich 1924.

BERTRAND, L. *La fin du Classicisme et le retour à l'Antique*. Paris 1897.

HAUTECŒUR, L. *Rome et la Renaissance de l'Antiquité*. Paris 1912.

RENOUVIER, J. *L'Art pendant la Révolution*. Paris 1863.

LOCQUIN, J. *Le retour de l'Antique dans l'Ecole anglaise et dans l'Ecole française avant David*. Paris 1922.

STENDHAL. *Mélange d'Art et de Littérature*. Paris 1867.

SILVESTRE, Th. *Histoire des Artistes vivants*. Paris 1855.

BAUDELAIRE, C. *Curiosités esthétiques*. Paris 1865.

MÉRIMÉE, P. *Salon de 1853*. Moniteur universel 1853.

BAUDELAIRE, C. *L'Art romantique*. Paris 1868.

CHESNEAU, E. *Peintres et Statuaires romantiques*. Paris 1880.

BANVILLE, Th. de. *Petites Etudes: les Souvenirs*. Paris 1882.

GONCOURT, E. and J. de. *Journal*. Paris 1887-1896.

MARX, R. *Etude sur l'Ecole française*. Paris 1903.

FAURE, E. *Histoire de l'Art*. Paris 1926.

BLANCHE, J. E. *La Troisième République*. Paris 1931.

MOLLETT, John W. *The Painters of Barbizon*. London 1890.

MICHEL, A. *Notes sur l'art moderne*. Paris 1896.

AUBRAT, O. *La peinture de genre en Angleterre de Hogarth au Préraphaélisme*. Paris 1934.

BRICE, T. and LANOE. *Histoire de l'école française du paysage*. Paris 1901.

BENOIST, BOUCHOT, BOUYER. *Histoire du paysage en France*. Paris 1908.

JOUIN, H. *Maîtres contemporains*. Paris 1887.

DURET, J. *Histoire des peintres impressionnistes*. Paris 1878.

AURIER, Ch. *L'impressionnisme*. Paris 1893.

VENTURI, L. *L'Impressionismo*. Milan 1935.

UHDE, W. *Les Impressionnistes*. Paris 1937.

WALDMANN, E. *Die Kunst des Realismus und des Impressionismus*. Berlin 1927.

PICA, V. *Gl'Impressionisti francesi*. Bergamo 1908.

MELLERIO, A. *L'exposition de 1900 et l'Impressionnisme*. Paris 1900.

MEIER-GRAEFE, J. *Der moderne Impressionnismus*. Berlin 1904.

MAUCLAIR, C. *L'impressionnisme*. Paris 1904.

LECOMTE, G. *L'art impressionniste*. Paris 1892.

KLINGSOR, T. *L'apport de l'Impressionnisme*. Paris 1928.

FÉNÉON, F. *Les Impressionnistes*. Paris (La Vogue) 1886.

DENIS, M. *Théories*. Paris 1912.

VENTURI, L. *Peintres modernes*. Paris 1941.

DORIVAL, B. *Les étapes de la peinture française contemporaine*. Paris 1945.

REWALD, John. *The History of Impressionism*. New York 1946.

SKIRA. *Histoire de la Peinture moderne*. Geneva 1949-1950.

WRIGHT, V. H. *Modern Painting*. New York 1915.

FRY, R. *Transformations*. London 1926.

MATHEY, F. J. *Modern Painting*. New York 1927.

PACH, W. *Masters of Modern Art*. New York 1929.

KLEIN, J. *Modern Masters*. New York 1938.

WILENSKI, R. H. *Modern French Painters*. New York 1940.

GENERAL INDEX

COLORPLATES